THE WORLD
Methodist
Movement

by

IVAN LEE HOLT

and

ELMER T. CLARK

Headquarters of
The Upper Room

The World's Most Widely Used Devotional Guide
AND
OTHER DEVOTIONAL LITERATURE

TABLE OF CONTENTS

IVAN LEE HOLT
President, World Methodist Council
The Upper Room annually gives a citation to some person chosen for outstanding leadership in the movement for world Christian fellowship. Bishop Holt will receive the citation in 1956.

Vice-President
Dr. Harold Roberts

Secretary
Dr. Elmer T. Clark

Secretary
The Rev. E. Benson Perkins

Chairman of the Executive Commmittee
Great Britain
The Rev. W. J. Noble

Treasurer
Edwin L. Jones

Chairman of the Executive Committee, U.S.A.
Dr. Oscar T. Olson

WORLD METHODIST COUNCIL
Officers

President: Bishop Ivan Lee Holt, 20 North Kingshighway, St. Louis, Missouri, U.S.A.

Vice-President: Dr. Harold Roberts, No. 2 College House, Richmond, Surrey, England

The Secretariat: Dr. Elmer T. Clark, Lake Junaluska, N.C., U.S.A.

Rev. E. Benson Perkins, 38 Belle Walk, Moseley, Birmingham 13, England

Treasurer: Mr. Edwin L. Jones, 1700 Brandon Road, Charlotte, North Carolina, U.S.A.

Associate Treasurer: Mr. L. A. Ellwood, 1 Watergate, Tudor Street, London, E.C. 4, England

Executive Committee

Chairman: Bishop Ivan Lee Holt, 20 North Kingshighway, St. Louis, Missouri, U.S.A.

Dr. Harold Roberts, No. 2, College House, Richmond, Surrey, England

Dr. Eric W. Baker, 1, Central Bldgs., Westminster, London, S.W.1

Dr. Elmer T. Clark, Lake Junaluska, N.C., U.S.A.

Bishop Bertram W. Doyle, 1702 Hieman Street, Nashville, Tennessee, U.S.A.

Dr. Dorothy Farrar, The College, Ilkley, Yorkshire, England

Professor A. Victor Murray, Cheshunt College, Cambridge, England

Rev. W. J. Noble, 59 Central Avenue, Herne Bay, Kent, England

Dr. Oscar Thomas Olson, 1919 East 107 Street, Cleveland, Ohio, U.S.A.

Hon. Charles C. Parlin, 20 Exchange Place, New York 5, U.S.A.

Rev. E. Benson Perkins, 38 Belle Walk, Moseley, Birmingham 13, England

Rev. Wilfred Easton, 25, Marylebone Rd., London N.W. 1, England

Mrs. Frank G. Brooks, Mount Vernon, Iowa, U.S.A.

Bishop S. L. Greene, 1212 Fountain Drive, S.W., Atlanta, Ga., U.S.A.

Bishop Odd Hagen, Langseleringen 41, Stockholm, Sweden

Mr. Edwin L. Jones, 1700 Brandon Rd., Charlotte, N.C., U.S.A.

Rev. G. I. Laurenson, Box 23 W., Auckland, C. 1, N.Z.

Rev. R. B. Lew, Park Rd., Burwood, N.S.W., Australia

Bishop Arthur J. Moore, 63 Auburn Rd., N.E., Atlanta 3, Ga., U.S.A.

Dr. T. Otto Nall, 740 Rush St., Chicago 11, Ill., U.S.A.

Dr. J. Manning Potts, 1908 Grand Avenue, Nashville, Tenn., U.S.A.

Rev. Wilfred Wade, 22, Pasture Rd., Wembley, Middlesex, England

Bishop W. J. Walls, 4736 S. Parkway, Chicago 16, Ill., U.S.A.

Dr. J. B. Webb, Methodist Central Hall, 66 Kruis St., Johannesburg, South Africa

Bishop Frederich Wunderlich, Frankfurt a.M.-Ginnheim, Ginnheimer Landstrasse, 180, Germany

PART I

Methodism and the Ecumenical Movement

by

IVAN LEE HOLT

CHAPTER I

THE ECUMENICAL MOVEMENT

IN THE *Ecumenical Review* for July, 1955, Dr. W. A. Visser 't Hooft discusses "Our Ecumenical Task in the Light of History." He suggests that there are three main approaches to the ecumenical problem. The first of these is the Erasmian, and these ideas are stressed in this approach:

(a) Church unity is possible and only possible on the basis of common agreement concerning a few necessary and fundamental points of doctrine.

It follows that:

(b) The short creedal formulations of the early Church are to be preferred, especially the Apostles' Creed, and new formulations concerning controversial points should be avoided. In all nonessentials there should be great freedom; no attempt should be made to impose detailed confessions of faith.

The second stream of ecumenical thinking can be described as the church-centered one. Its concern is not in the first place with doctrinal propositions or with individual experience, but with God's design in calling His people.

We may summarize its main characteristics in the following way:

(a) The design of God is to gather a people which is His own people and exists to glorify Him. This Church of God, which is at the same time the Body of Christ, is by its very nature a single, united community.

It follows that:

(b) It is the task of the faithful to manifest that given unity in the world and that

(c) This unity is not the unity of the lowest common denomi-

9

nator, but rather that in which the faith is taught and believed in its wholeness and fullness.

With the third stream of ecumenical thought we enter into a different atmosphere. While the central concept of the Erasmians is assent to doctrine, however simplified, and the central concept of the second tradition is the Church, the third group, the Pietists, are concerned with the Christian life. We can summarize their ecumenical position thus:

(a) Christianity is first of all an individual experience and a life; all Christians who are truly saved belong together, whatever their church allegiance.

It follows that:

(b) Church and doctrine are only relevant in so far as they contribute to individual conversion and that

(c) Every Christian is called to participate in the common task of evangelism and mission.

The Secretary of the World Council, Dr. Visser 't Hooft, feels that the Erasmian concept is no longer a challenge to us. In his opinion our ecumenical task today is to reconcile or integrate the other two approaches because each of them needs the other. As we face this task we need to keep in mind the history of the past generation in the ecumenical movement. It was in 1910 that the missionary leaders of the church had their great conference in Edinburgh. This is generally regarded as the beginning of the modern ecumenical movement. Since then the International Missionary Council has brought together Protestant leaders in Jerusalem, Tambaram, and Whitby. One of the great organizational problems is to relate the International Missionary Council and the World Council of Churches as the effort is made to find a place in the larger church for a combined objective of mission and unity.

When World War I was over and hatred had separated nations and their churches, there was a conviction in the minds of some churchmen that the churches must find a common objective if the wounds of war were to be healed. In one of the neutral nations,

Sweden, Archbishop Söderblom issued a call to the churches to send representatives to a conference on life and work at Stockholm. That was in 1925.

The Conference in Stockholm was a Conference on Life and Work. Here the representatives of many churches sought to work out a program to which churches could subscribe. It was known that there were many differences in belief and doctrine on which common agreement could not be reached, but it was thought that the churches could undertake tasks in common to rebuild a broken world. Never had the churches of the world been brought so close together, and the inspiration of that meeting is still a vital force in Protestantism.

Bishop Charles H. Brent, of the Protestant Episcopal Church in the United States, was much interested in seeking some agreements on doctrine. He was responsible for the calling of the Conference on Faith and Order at Lausanne in 1927. Most of the members of the churches, who know anything about this Conference, remember that it was impossible to hold a joint service of Holy Communion and that, at the conclusion of the Conference, there had to be several such services. However, it became apparent that the churches did agree in many fundamentals of belief. It was decided there, as it had been at Stockholm, to hold a subsequent Conference.

Just before the outbreak of World War II, in 1937 the second Conference on Life and Work was held at Oxford, and a few days later the second Conference on Faith and Order was held at Edinburgh. At Oxford there was much discussion of the relationship of church and society in view of the rise of Naziism and Fascism. The duty of the Christian in his relationship to the state was stressed, and it was decided to seek a merger with the Conference on Faith and Order in a plan to create a World Council of Churches. At the Edinburgh Conference it was apparent that there were differences in doctrinal emphasis, but some surprising things happened under the leadership of the Holy Spirit. The Commission on "The Grace of Our Lord Jesus Christ" was able to work out a statement which se-

11

cured the unanimous approval of the members of the Commission. This was afterwards approved by the whole Conference. At the close of the Conference the Archbishop of York led a great service in St. Giles Cathedral. In view of the past history of conflicts in Scotland it was a thrilling experience to all present to have an Anglican Archbishop in the pulpit of the cathedral church of Presbyterianism. He summoned all present to remember that while grateful to their fathers for a heritage of great convictions, they were coming into a new day in which they and their children must come into a new fellowship. Between the Conferences at Oxford and Edinburgh there was a service in St. Paul's Cathedral in London where the Archbishop of Canterbury preached on the text, "Speak unto the children of Israel that they go forward." In that service there were about one hundred denominations from forty different lands, and in the procession that filed into the Cathedral the representatives of those churches wore their ecclesiastical vestments. Orthodox and Protestant clergy and hundreds of people on sidewalks and steps watched the colorful procession move into the Cathedral. In his sermon, the Archbishop interpreted the new co-operation that had come, and those who were present sensed the reality of the larger Church.

At Edinburgh it was voted to join in the movement for a World Council of Churches, and before World War II it was possible to set up a Provisional Committee of the World Council of Churches. In the summer of 1939, as the war seemed imminent, the Provisional Committee called together in Geneva a group of some forty representatives of churches from over the world to exert an effort to prevent the outbreak of war. That Conference formulated an address to the foreign ministers of the great nations and also worked out a statement on "The Duty of Christians in Time of War." When it became apparent that war was coming, in spite of all efforts to prevent it, the members of the Conference hastily left Geneva and hurried to their homes. I went to England to preach on that last Sunday in August in a Presbyterian Church at Birkenhead. Never will I forget the feverish excitement of those days and the uncertainty about reaching home. We sailed on the *Queen Mary*, and it was blacked out at night while crossing the ocean because it was rumored that a German submarine was following it. While we were at sea, the *Athenia* was sunk and the Germans moved into Poland. By the time we reached New York the War had begun.

The Provisional Committee was able to render a great service during the War by keeping in touch with churches in warring lands and providing chaplains for prisoners of war. It was a providential thing that this Committee had been organized, and there is no way to emphasize too strongly its service during the tragic days of war. In the neutral land of Switzerland it was able to maintain some form of contact with churches across the warring world.

The War was over in 1945, but it was not until 1948 that the Provisional Committee could organize the First Assembly of the World Council of Churches. This was held in the city of Amsterdam just before Queen Wilhelmina passed on to her daughter the responsibility of governing, and Queen Juliana was crowned immediately after the close of the Assembly. The streets of the city were gayly decorated, and the lights were turned on the canals for the first time in years. It was a time of rejoicing for the people of Holland, and it was a time of gratitude to God for the representatives of the churches to come together from the ends of the earth. There were services of worship led by men and women of different traditions, and there were discussions which stressed both differences and agreements. Before the end of the Assembly it was apparent that in the Protestant world there were in Protestantism both a Catholic mind and a Protestant mind. There were some sharp differences of opinion about the relationship of Christianity and Communism. In spite of these differences there was real progress in the development of a sense of fellowship. Plans were made for another Assembly and a Central Committee was formed to carry on in the interim.

The first meeting of the Central Committee was held at Chichester in England. Almost all the ninety members of the Committee were present. The Bishop of Chichester was chairman of the Committee and the host of the meeting. It was possible to consider the work of different committees and to further stabilize the work of the Council. The second meeting of the Central Committee was held in Toronto in 1950. There a resolution was passed endorsing the resistance to aggression in Korea. Perhaps the most important action of that session was the consideration of the Church and the churches. It was a very thoughtful attempt to arrive at some understanding as to the relation of the member churches to the larger Church, and that discussion has had its influence on subsequent meetings.

The Central Committee met in Rolle, Switzerland, in 1951 and in Lucknow, India, in January of 1953. These two meetings were devoted largely to a discussion of plans for the Second Assembly. It was decided to hold that Assembly in Evanston, Illinois, U.S.A., in 1954; and an agreement was reached as to the apportionment of delegates. There was long discussion of the report of the Theological Commission and of the theme for the Assembly. It was suggested that the theme should be "The Crucified Lord, the Hope of the World." As a substitute it was moved that the theme should be "The Crucified and Risen Lord, the Hope of the World." After a long discussion, the decision was reached to make the theme, "Christ, the Hope of the World."

During the meeting at Lucknow, the churches of Asia had a chance to bring before the Committee the problems which Christianity faces in the Orient. It was most helpful to the representatives of the Western churches to have this point of view so ably presented. Not since the Conference at Tambaram, before World War II, was there such an opportunity for the younger churches to stress matters which seemed so important to them. They indicated a degree of impatience with the older churches in the slowness of their progress toward unity.

The Second Assembly of the World Council of Churches met at

Evanston in the late summer and early fall of 1954. Evanston and Northwestern University were generous hosts. The President of the United States came to address the Assembly. There were thousands of visitors, and the Assembly had very wide publicity in the American press. There were many differences of opinion, even in the interpretation of the theme. However, it was apparent that the frank presentation of differences was necessary and even an aid in arriving eventually at deeper understandings. The Service of Holy Communion at the First Methodist Church was attended by several thousand, and participating in it were representatives of most of the great church families in the United States. The rite of The Methodist Church in the United States was followed in the service, and it may be many years before another Methodist Service of Holy Communion is held at an Assembly of the World Council. It was my privilege to lead in a Methodist Service of Holy Communion for the Central Committee in the Chapel of Isabella Thoburn College in Lucknow, India. For Methodism those two services are historic. Two Methodists have been on the Presidium of the World Council, Bishop G. Bromley Oxnam between Amsterdam and Evanston, and Bishop S. U. Barbieri, since Evanston. In the early part of 1956 the Executive Committee of the Central Committee held a very influential meeting in Australia. The Central Committee itself will meet in Budapest in the summer of 1956, and the next Assembly will probably be held in Ceylon. Thus the influence of the World Council is extended to different sections of the world. Within the year 1956 there have been interesting exchanges of visits between the Orthodox Church of Russia and the western churches.

Without any question the most significant achievement of both Amsterdam and Evanston was the promotion of acquaintance and fellowship. Men and women from every section of the Christian world came to know each other and prayed together. In memory lingers the atmosphere of comradeship and a recognition of oneness in Christ. It will be a long time before there can be a union of widely separated churches, but there has come in these two great Assemblies a new appreciation of the Church of our Lord Jesus Christ. To that appreciation Methodism has made a great contribution.

Before the end of World War II the British Methodist Conference appointed a committee to prepare a report on the Message and Mission of Methodism. After three years of study the Committee reported to the Conference Session of 1946, and the report is as fine a statement on the message and mission of our church as has been written. It concerns itself with the message of the Church, the witness of Methodism, and the Church in action in modern society. It stresses for our day some facts Methodists should note:

(1) The picture of men and women in large numbers hungering for the true Bread of Heaven exists only in the imagination of those who are unconsciously afraid to face brute facts;

(2) It would be sheer folly to imagine that there is no longer any divergence between science and religion. There is a conflict between the Christian faith and the attitude which is based on the assumption, so widespread in our day, that the scientific method is the sole means of ascertaining truth.

(3) It would be foolish to contend that the message and method of John Wesley in the Eighteenth Century should be repeated in the Twentieth Century, though his gospel is valid today.

(4) Methodism has no doctrines that cannot be found in the rich heritage of the Universal Church. The Methodist witness to the gospel is none the less distinctive, and it would be tragedy, if and when we attain one fellowship, to find the Methodist emphasis lacking. The Church is one and its unity derives from the common relationship of its members to Christ. The marks of Methodism in the Universal Church are the emphasis on salvation by faith, conversion, assurance, perfection in love, and fellowship. Early Methodism knew nothing of solitary religion nor was it aware of any fundamental conflict between personal religion and life in the Communion of Saints. The quest of holiness is both individual and social. For that reason Methodism is by nature evangelistic and mis-

sionary, and Methodism must ever be seeking the end of divisions in Christ's Holy Church.

With this clearly-stated concept in mind of the Methodist message and mission, it is my purpose now to consider briefly the Methodist Ecumenical Movement.

After his conversion John Wesley went more frequently than ever to the Anglican Service of Holy Communion, and in a real sense he was more of a churchman. There was a desire in most of the Reformers to maintain or recover one Holy and Apostolic Church, but I believe it is a defensible position to insist that Wesley was the most ecumenically minded of all the great reformers. Methodism has been true to his historical concept of fellowship when it has co-operated with other Christian bodies in seeking One Fold, when there is One Shepherd.

The Methodist Ecumenical Movement dates from resolutions in the General Conference of the Methodist Episcopal Church and in the Annual Conference of British Methodism between the years 1876 and 1880. The first Ecumenical Conference of Methodism was held in City Road Chapel, London, in 1881; the second in Washington in 1891; the third in London in 1901; the fourth in Toronto in 1911; the fifth at Central Hall in London in 1921; the sixth in Atlanta in 1931; the seventh at Trinity Church in Springfield, Massachusetts, in 1947, and the eighth at Oxford in 1951. It has been my privilege to be in all of the Conferences since that of 1921 in London. At other places in this book will be presented the significance of these Conferences. Suffice it to say here that the early Conferences were primarily devoted to addresses and fellowship.

At the Conference in Springfield in 1947 there was set up a real world organization, since it was apparent that Methodism had a contribution to make to the rebuilding of a world that was so sadly broken to pieces in World War II. The Conference at Oxford developed still further the world organization. As an indication of the growing realization of our oneness as Methodists, I recall some personal experiences of the summer of 1955. In the early days of

June that year the Executive Committee of the World Methodist Conference met at Edgehill College in Belfast, Northern Ireland. There we made plans for the next World Methodist Conference, and it was most inspiring for American Methodists to have contact there with Methodist origins. On Sunday before the opening of the Irish Conference I preached in Donegall Square Methodist Church, and behind me was a great chancel window, placed there in memory of Philip Embury, Barbara Heck, and Robert Strawbridge by Methodists in the United States. Americans may continue to argue whether the first Methodist Church was organized in New York or Baltimore, but they know that those who organized the first Methodist Societies in those cities, as well as Philadelphia, were Irish Methodists.

Then the Reverend E. Benson Perkins and I went to Bristol for one of the most thrilling experiences of my years as President of the World Methodist Council, the Dedication of the Memorial Gates at the New Room. Never can I forget the privilege of standing in Wesley's pulpit at Bristol, nor the courtesies of the Lord Mayor and the Council, who rendered so great a service to the Methodism of Bristol and the world in providing such conspicuous and beautiful entrance ways to one of Methodism's real shrines.

I went on to London, and at City Road Chapel I dedicated the tablet which expresses appreciation of the gift to the Chapel of thirty thousand dollars by American Methodists. Two years ago I dedicated the cross on the altar, given also by an American Methodist Church. These contacts serve to relate all Methodism to its British Shrines, and to prepare us the better for our next World Conference.

During these recent years there have been many contacts between our British Methodist leaders and the various sections of World Methodism. One of the most significant of these movements has been the developing fellowship between the Methodists of Europe. As far back as 1939 there was held in Copenhagen a Conference of European Methodists. There were present several American Methodists because several of the European Methodist Churches owe their origin to the missionary activity of American Methodists. The sermon in that Conference was preached by the President of the British Methodist Conference. Methodism, which had its origin in the British Isles and went on to encircle the globe, came back to Europe to strengthen Methodist ties there.

In other Communions there have developed world movements. It has been my privilege in recent years to attend the World Lutheran Conference at Hanover, Germany, and the World Presbyterian Conference at Princeton, New Jersey. The Anglicans, the Baptists, the Congregationalists, and the Disciples have world organizations, but no one of them has been more effectively organized than the World Methodist Movement. In all of this development the Methodist Churches of the world have been closely related to the World Council of Churches, and it is now apparent that world denominational fellowships can add strength to the Ecumenical Movement, without detracting from it.

There are other World Organizations like the Y.M.C.A. and the Y.W.C.A. and the Student Christian Movement which enrich world-wide fellowship. After the close of World War I the World Alliance for International Friendship held some very significant Conferences in Europe. As a matter of fact, one of the most successful was held in Cambridge as far back as 1931. Having financial resources through its contact with the Church Peace Union in America, this organization not only contributed to understanding among the churches but had a very real part in the organization of the Conferences at Stockholm and Lausanne. Then the World Sunday School Convention, which became the International Council of Religious Education, has made its contribution through very inspiring world gatherings. Thus has the Ecumenical Movement become the most significant development in church life during this century.

CHAPTER II

METHODISM AND ECUMENICAL CHRISTIANITY

One of the scholarly church historians in the United States, a member of another denomination, recently said to me, "John Wesley was the most ecumenically minded of all the great reformers." Frequently the Protestant Reformation is interpreted as a break with Catholic Christendom. As a matter of fact, many leaders in the Reformation Movement were so deeply concerned about the unity of the church that they interpreted their organizations as essential steps in the promotion of unity. The catholicity of John Wesley's movement is revealed not only in his hesitancy to break with the Church of England but in his very great concern for the fellowship of those whose hearts are one even though they differ in their opinions.

Through the years of Methodist history there has always been a zeal for co-operation with other communions. When the General Conference of the Methodist Episcopal Church, South, met in Birmingham, Alabama, in 1938, the Committee on Church Relations presented as its first report a declaration of its desire for a Protestant union. Its immediate concern was the union of three Methodist Churches, but it did not desire to lose sight of a larger union in its undertaking of the immediate task.

Not only has there been this zeal for co-operation in Methodism, but there are catholic concepts of religious rites. In the service of Holy Communion all are invited who are truly sorry for their sins, are in love and charity with their neighbors, and intend to lead a new life. In administering the rite of baptism, any of the historical methods may be used as the candidate prefers. It has never been possible to get the approval of a General Conference for the writing of a Methodist Creed to which all must subscribe. The creed used in Methodist Churches is that which is common to all churches in Christendom.

Furthermore, Methodism has both approaches to religion. It was generally accepted at the Edinburgh Conference on Faith and Order in 1937 that the two approaches to religion made by the churches of Christendom are the historical approach and the psychological approach. The Methodist Church has its ritual services, taken by John Wesley from the *Book of Common Prayer* of the Church of England. Some of the prayers in those services are very old and go back to earlier centuries in the history of the Christian Church. Not only does Methodism lay claim to the great traditions of the church through the centuries before the Reformation, but in its services it incorporates prayers that grew out of the religious experiences of saints of other days. In a very true sense of the word, the Methodist Church is a ritualistic church and has the historical approach. On the other hand, the Methodist movement is traced to the heart-warming experience of John Wesley. Its witness is the witness of the love of God and the saving grace of our Lord Jesus Christ. All-important is the religious experience of the believer.

The Challenges to Methodism

One who is conscious of the zeal for co-operation in Methodism, its catholic concepts of religious rites, and its two approaches to religion, feels that God has put into the hands of the people called Methodist very great gifts. These gifts can be used for the advancement of the Kingdom in the critical days of this post-war world.

Recent years have brought challenges to Methodists in every section of the world. As illustrations of our unlimited opportunities and our extending horizons, let me take you to three areas on three different continents. The first Protestant leader from the outside world to enter Poland after World War II was the Methodist bishop in Europe. He was assured by the Polish government that Protestant missionaries would be welcomed, and there gathered around him not only Methodist preachers but also preachers from the older Protestant churches in Poland. The German Lutheran Church was strong in Western Poland before World War II, but most of its ministers and members had crossed the border into Germany. The Reformed Church had lost buildings and congregations at a time when it seemed possible to bring our Methodist work into contact with older Protestant Churches. Those same churches then turned to Methodism for guidance and leadership. Now that a decade has passed since those crucial days, the pattern for Protestant organization in Poland is not clear, though Methodism seems to continue under native leadership, having taken over great church buildings of other communions.

In Japan the Church of Christ has been reorganized. Before the war between Japan and the United States, a deputation of Japanese churchmen came to our country to acquaint American Protestants with this new religious movement. The members of this deputation insisted that union had come both under pressure of the government and through the desire of leaders in all denominations. As short a time ago as January, 1938, I suggested to a Missionary Conference of the Methodist Episcopal Church, South, in the light of my experience in the Orient, that the time was fast approaching when we must make a total Christian advance in Eastern Asia. Very few members of the conference agreed with me, but in less than ten years the Executive Committee of the Board of Missions of the Methodist Church voted to co-operate with other Protestant churches in America in that kind of an advance. The mother churches in Anglo-Saxon nations can never forget the appeal of the younger churches in the Madras Conference. The movement toward church union is so pronounced in the mission fields that Boards of Missions cannot stand in the way of it, even if they should desire to do so.

In Latin America I had some amazing experiences in 1945. While the Roman Catholic Church is vigorously opposed to the Protestant missionary enterprise and does not know the meaning of religious liberty in our interpretation of it, it is true that in some of the republics of Central and South America Protestants enjoy almost as much freedom as though they were majority groups. Many pictures are in my mind as I think of that journey through South America. One of the vivid ones is of a group of two hundred students gathered on a station platform to bid me farewell, as I left a town in the interior of Brazil. They sang heartily "Brazil for Christ," the hymn of Evangelical Christianity. I knew that those students were in our Methodist school over the protest of bishop and priest; I knew that eighty per cent of them were still nominally Roman Catholic; but at the same time they sang the great hymn of Protestantism without creating the least disturbance in a crowd of five hundred people in and around the station.

It may be a long time before we have any large Protestant movement in Latin America, but the way seems open in many countries. In more than one republic the opposition is more anti-American than it is anti-Protestant. In the matter of church organization a real challenge and a problem are presented in a country like Mexico. A decade ago the Boards of Missions of several denominations in the United States divided the Mexican territory in a fine comity agreement. The Methodist Episcopal Church, South, was given the territory just south of the Rio Grande. The Methodist Episcopal Church had the section around Mexico City. After the union of these two churches and the organization of the Methodist Church in Mexico, it was found that there is a great stretch of territory between the two sections of Methodist influence. The Methodist Church of Mexico now feels that the comity agreement is outmoded and desires to work out its relationship with other Protestant denominations through the National Christian Council of Mexico. A later trip to Mexico and South America confirms earlier impressions.

These glimpses of situations around the world reveal new problems in church administration, but they present also great challenges to church leadership. It is a well-known fact that three-fourths of the Protestant missionary enterprise is carried by churches in Great Britain and the United States. Of this responsibility the Methodist Church carries one-sixteenth. Since probably three-fourths of the people in the world are non-Christian, there is still such a task of evangelism as to stagger the imagination unless the churches of Christendom work together. In the five great nations which led the Allied cause to victory in World War II, there are approximately 850 million people, and in all probability not more than 150 million could be called Christian. Not only is it beyond the strength of any one church to Christianize the world, but it is not conceivable that such a task can be accomplished without far more cooperation than has heretofore been known.

The Ecumenical Movement in Methodism

Conscious of these and other challenges after the war, the Methodist Ecumenical Commission planned for an Ecumenical Conference to meet in the United States from September 24 to October 1 in 1947. The first Ecumenical Conference was held in 1881, and at intervals of ten years other conferences have been held until World War II made impossible a conference scheduled for Oxford, England, in 1941. In preliminary conferences of representatives of American Methodism and British Methodism some agreements were unanimously reached. These proposals were made to the Ecumenical Conference of 1947, and approved by that body.

(a) The preceding Ecumenical Conference had brought Methodists together for consultation and reading of thoughtful papers. The post-war world situation made it imperative for any subsequent conferences to bring the influence of Methodism to bear on the solution of world problems. This meant that we must find ways to work together and be content no longer with the exchange of opinions and with fraternization.

(b) Heretofore there had been an Eastern Section of the Ecumenical Conference, including all the churches which stem

24

from British Methodism, and a Western Section, including all the churches that stem from American Methodism. For a long time we were conscious of the inadequacy of such organization because churches in territory close to American shores were in the Eastern Section, and churches in China and India were in the Western Section. Furthermore it was almost impossible to think of Anglo-Saxon churches in Methodism dividing the world between them. Independent Methodist Churches had been organized in Brazil, Japan, Korea, and Mexico. Central conferences had been set up in various parts of the world, and it was perfectly apparent that world-wide Methodism must have a different form of ecumenical organization. Instead of two sections there could be six or seven sections formed along geographical lines.

(c) Through its far-flung missionary program, Methodism is found in almost every section of the world. For this reason, Ecumenical Methodism can exert a tremendous influence in the solution of the world's economic and social problems if a plan can be devised through which it can function.

(d) Since the First Assembly of the World Council of Churches in 1948 there have been two points of view with reference to continuation of denominational world fellowships. Some have felt that since each denomination has membership in the World Council of Churches, its own ecumenical organization should be discontinued. Others have felt that the denominational world fellowship can be built into the organization of the World Council.

It is perfectly apparent that the Lutheran Churches of the world intend to continue their fellowship. At a meeting of the British Council of Churches after the war, Bishop Berggrav of Norway said in substance: "While the churches of Norway came to experience a new fellowship under Nazi persecution, it is also true

25

that the creed of our Lutheran Church meant much more than it ever meant before. I want to see the walls between the churches maintained though I would like to see them low enough for us to look over the top." That attitude is not the one many of us would like to see prevail, but it is perfectly apparent that we are not ready to discard all denominational loyalties.

In an article in *Christendom* some years ago, it was my suggestion that the World Council could have two sections, an Assembly and an Executive Council. Following the scheme of political organizations, the Assembly might have representatives elected by the constituent denominations. The Executive Council might have representatives elected by the Assembly and in addition representatives of area and denominational ecumenical groups. It is my conviction that we need to preserve all the gains in fellowship that we have built up through the years. That plan has not been adopted, but some such scheme may yet be considered.

Methodism and the World Council

It goes without saying that the Methodist Church will continue to support the World Council of Churches. While the leadership of that organization has often been placed in the hands of European churchmen, the American churches have furnished a great part of the financial support. Through the war years, and since, much of the responsibility for maintaining the World Council organization in Geneva has fallen to American churches. The Methodist Church has been a generous supporter and an interested member of the World Council. There is no question about its interest in world co-operation. In each and every world conference during the last twenty-five years the Methodist Church has sent large delegations and has given hearty support.

The Oxford Conference of 1951

In 1951, one thousand Methodists from all over the world came to Oxford for the World Methodist Conference. In the business sessions of the Conference the organization of world Methodism was further developed, and after the close of that Conference it was evident that, for the first time since the days of John Wesley, the Methodists around the world were one people. Shortly before his death, John Wesley wrote to one of his preachers in America, "Lose no opportunity to proclaim to people everywhere the fact that the Methodists are one pepole." What we had dreamed of doing before Oxford, we accomplished there. The officers elected by that conference became truly the leaders of all the Methodist Churches of the world.

Methodism and Church Union in the United States

When one turns from the world scene to think about national problems, he is aware again of the fact that there is a great need for co-operation. It is a matter of rejoicing that Methodist union has worked out so successfully in the United States. The Evangelical Church and the United Brethren Church have united their forces, and it is my conviction that The Methodist Church ought in the near future to extend an invitation to this united church to join with us in the creation of a still larger church.

In any discussion of Protestant union in the United States, it is natural to think of churches uniting which have common doctrines and common policies. It would seem logical for the Disciples and the Northern Baptists to unite. It has always seemed logical to me for the Methodist and the Protestant Episcopal churches to unite because they have ritual services and polities that are so strikingly similar.

For five years The Methodist Church and the Protestant Episcopal Church have been discussing union, and just now we are considering a very interesting proposal that might lead to approaches to intercommunion. After the last joint meeting of the commissions representing the two churches, we had a conference of bishops at which eleven Protestant Episcopal bishops and eight Methodist bishops discussed the proposals for intercommunion. All bishops there present were strongly of the opinion that we must have another meeting soon.

As chairman of the Conference on Church Union, I am deeply interested in the blueprint we have drawn for a larger Protestant church in the United States, formed through a merger of the seven denominations which sent delegates to the Conference at Greenwich, Connecticut, on Church Union. I spoke at the last meeting of the Executive Committee of the World Methodist Council on these two union efforts in American Methodism because in our world organization we have agreed to keep one another informed in case any Methodist church in any land plans a union within the nation. The British Methodist Conference at its session in July, 1955, proposed conversations between British Methodists and the Church of England, partly inspired to take that action by my report on Episcopalian-Methodist negotiations in the United States. In other sections of the Methodist world unions are being discussed.

Within the past six months I have journeyed sixty thousand miles and more through the West Indies, the British Isles, the Continent of Europe, Australia, New Zealand, the Fiji Islands, Hawaii, South America, and Central America, drawing Methodists together; and everywhere I found Methodists co-operating with other communions. In half a dozen of the areas visited there were discussions of union with other churches.

The Task of Methodism

As the World Council of Churches and the International Missionary Council discuss co-operation and missions, The Methodist Church with its missionary passion understands both the emphasis on union and the emphasis on mission. As it stresses these two phases of expression in the life of the church, Methodism may aid in bringing to the World Council of Churches a deeper sense of the importance of mission. The Methodist task is the task of Protestant Christianity, but the genius of Methodism can lead to a clearer understanding of both union and mission.

The Witness of Methodism

Methodism has a witness to bear in these days. It is so easy to become entangled in God's judgments. When we listened in silence to the report of Japan's surrender as it came into our homes by radio, we had a feeling of having found seats in God's judgment hall. We know also that even the victorious nations have been brought to the bar of judgment. It is so easy for us to embrace the theology which speaks only of crisis and sins and talks about man's inadequacy. In such an hour I cannot forget that Methodism's great undertaking is to see that no one misses the grace of God. Before leaving England in the summer of 1948, I spent several days in the home of a British layman. He was the vice-president of the British Conference. In our conversation on the last night he told me of his plan to speak at a great service in Cornwall on Whitmonday. Since the day when John Wesley spoke on Whitmonday to a group of miners in Cornwall, the Methodists have had a service on the spot where he stood. The British layman said to me:

"You have seen pictures of the miners listening to Wesley and they had tears coursing down their cheeks. These have been thought of as tears of repentance. It is true that John Wesley spoke to those miners about their sins and by his powerful sermons he convicted them and brought them to penitence. Those tears were also tears of joy because the preacher told these social outcasts, who would not be welcome at the King's Court or in the great houses of England, that they were sons of the King of Heaven. Not only did he convince these forgotten men of God's interest but he also convinced them of God's love. It is my conviction that we would not hold that service year after year if Wesley had talked only about a man's sin. We hold it because Wesley talked about God's love."

How often have I thought of that when in a world in revolt communism claims to throw the only lifeline to the underprivileged masses of the world!

One of the churches in England destroyed by German bombs was the historic church of St. Clement Danes on the Strand. A

29

friend told me that he was walking along the Strand on the Sunday after the church was destroyed. He saw a woman climbing over the rubble with a vase of flowers in her hand. She placed it on the only corner of the altar still standing. That is the kind of faith that Methodism seeks to keep alive in the world. Important as it is for Methodism to promote church union and Christian unity, it is equally important that it should in Ecumenical Christianity bear its historical witness to the grace of our Lord Jesus Christ and the Love of God. When co-operation and zeal to heal the broken body of our Lord have done their work, it will be found that a great contribution of Methodism to world Christianity will be the warming of its heart.

We face the future not as a church which identifies itself with the Kingdom, nor one which feels itself a small remnant of the faithful in perpetual conflict with an alien universe. "Our hope sees beyond the years and we live in this demanding present under the everlasting assurance of God's love." Close each day with the entry "Adelante," beloved Church, that at the beginning of each day may be heard God's voice: "Turn you, take your journey and go."

This does not mean that we support the philosophy of a long-run optimism by which we believe in the certain progressive elimination of sin and evil. We must resist the temptation to accept that philosophy as we reject the pessimism of neo-orthodoxy. We voice our faith for the future in these words: "Christian hope for human society is based on the fact of God's creative and redemptive working which is woven through the whole fabric of life. . . . Today to establish the City of Man on anything else than faith in God is to build on quicksand." Those words of Daniel Day Williams set forth our faith, as do these sentences: "Paul's faith that love hopeth all things is not sentimentality. It is the affirmation which Christian faith must make about what it means to trust in God." "For we are saved by hope." "If God be for us, who can be against us?" "Tribulation worketh patience; and patience, experience; and experience, hope." That is the faith and must be the faith of Methodism.

The author of the Epistle to the Romans was a realist. He never buried his head in the sand, but looked straight at the facts of life. No one could accuse him of shallow optimism. The pain and tragedy of the world were ever before him, and no theologian was ever more vividly aware of the sinfulness of man or the prevalence of evil. "The whole creation groaneth and travaileth in pain together until now." Yet Paul was so sure of the transforming power of God, through Christ in human life and in this world, that he could write with confidence: "We are saved by hope."

In an admirable biography of Christopher Columbus called *The Admiral of the Ocean Seas*, we are told that the explorer often recorded in his diary the prayer: "May Jesus Christ go with us on the way." Then at the close of each day, whether the sailing was pleasant or the sea was rough, whether the crew was co-operative or mutinous, he wrote at the end of the entry the word *Adelante*, "Forward."

> "Lead on, O King Eternal,
>   The day of march has come;
> Henceforth in fields of conquest
>   Thy tents shall be our home."

CHAPTER III

METHODISM AND CHURCH UNIONS

W HENEVER Protestant Union is under discussion, it will be found that the Methodist Church is one of the interested groups. Within the United States of America there have been at least twenty unions of churches within the last generation. In this country and in the rest of the world the Methodist Church has been seeking always to promote closer fellowships between the separate churches.

The most widely discussed unions in which Methodists have participated are those which resulted in the United Church of Canada in 1925, the United Church of South India in 1947, both interdenominational, the Union of Methodist Churches of Great Britain in 1932, and the Union of Methodist Churches in the United States in 1939, both within the Methodist family. In the negotiations that led to the formation of the United Church of Canada, the Methodist Church played a very important role. The Congregationalists and the Presbyterians had an equally deep interest, but the Methodist Church was the largest of the uniting churches. I can remember so well that the leaders of that movement used to say, "We were able to bring about Union because Union had actually taken place in the fellowship of the members of the separate churches." So far as Canada was concerned, it was possible to reach doctrinal agreements and agreements as to church polity because churches of the three denominations had learned to live together, and were appreciative of a challenge that was too great for any single denomination to meet. While some of the Presbyterianisms did not go into the Union and have maintained a continuing church, there is an ever deepening conviction that it was God's spirit that led these churches to become one. The work of the years since has demonstrated that it was a wise course, and very few people in the

United Church of Canada would want to return to the old order.

The United Church of Canada maintains affiliation with the world organizations of the Congregational, the Methodist, and the Presbyterian churches. It continues to be a part of the World Methodist Council. In each of the World Conferences of Methodism since 1925, the United Church of Canada has had its representatives, and in this relationship it has set an example for other United Churches.

The most interesting thing about the United Church of South India is that the Anglican Church was a party to the discussions and the Union. That Church came into being just as the Methodists were assembling for their Seventh Ecumenical Conference in Springfield, Massachusetts, and the first business of that Conference was the ordering of a resolution of congratulations and good wishes to the Church of South India. The Methodist Church which went into that Union was British, the American Methodists in India being related to the present scheme for a United Church in North India.

While there is some difference of opinion among Anglicans as to the recognition of the Church of South India, there is no doubt about the fact that this is the most significant Union of our time. One of the most inspiring services at the Assembly of the World Council of Churches in Evanston was the Communion Service of the Church of South India, held in the First Methodist Church in Evanston. The ritual of that service embodied practices of the uniting churches, but also some practices from the rituals of the Church in the early Christian centuries. Of course, it was an open Communion, and all Christians of all churches were invited to communicate. It seemed to those present that the celebrants were not only conscious of their new and deeper fellowship, but also of the fact that they had established a fellowship with early Christians before the divisions in the Christian world. In this first decade of its life, the United Church of South India is teaching its people to forget the differences that once separated them, and it will not be many years before those members will think only of their one Church.

In view of the relationship of the Anglican Church and in view of discussions in other lands between Anglicans and Methodists, this church may be pointing the way to a reunion of Methodists with an Anglican Church out of which the Methodist Movement came. The next Lambeth Conference will be of great interest not only to Anglicans but also to Methodists. Should that Conference give its full endorsement to the South India Union, the way would certainly be opened for possible approaches to intercommunion between Anglicans and Methodists. Not since the announcement of the Quadrilateral from Lambeth has there been a more important pronouncement than will be made at the coming Conference.

The Union which brought the largest numbers from separate churches is that of the union within the Methodist family of the United States. The Methodist Episcopal Church, the Methodist Episcopal Church, South, and the Methodist Protestant Church united in a great Conference at Kansas City, Missouri, in 1939. The road to union was a long one. The Methodist Protestant Church had broken away from Episcopal Methodism over the issue of bishops in the Church. The Methodist Episcopal Church and the Methodist Episcopal Church, South, had separated through the growing tensions between the northern and southern sections of the United States over slavery. There were other issues involved in both of these separations. For example, the Methodist Protestant Church laid an increasing emphasis on the importance of the local church. Between the Methodist Episcopal Church and the Methodist Episcopal Church, South, there developed in 1844 quite different concepts of the function and office of the bishop.

In the long road to union there were Commissions on Comity which sought to settle disputes over property. There were interchanges of fraternal messages. There was a joint hymnal, published a generation before the actual union of the churches. There were also Commissions of Unification which proposed and brought to a vote certain plans for union before the final plan was approved at the Uniting Conference in Kansas City. At that Conference the Methodist Protestants who were present as delegates elected two of their number as bishops in the United Church, thus surrendering a conviction that was largely responsible for the early separation. At that Conference a process of harmonizing the polity and programs of the separate churches was begun, each church contributing from its own experience procedures which had been worked out over the years.

No one who was present in Kansas City can never forget the emotional experiences associated with the consummation of that Union, and through the years since there has emerged a church with an entity of its own, a church greater than would be represented by the sum total of the members of the uniting churches.

Some seven years before this merger the Primitive Methodist Church, the United Methodist Church, and the Wesleyan Methodist Church in Great Britain had united in a great conference at Royal Albert Hall in London. In many ways this was a more significant union than that which took place in the United States because there were many communities in the British Isles which had all three of these churches. In the United States the Methodist Episcopal Church functioned largely in the northern section of the country, and the Methodist Episcopal Church, South, in the southern section of the country. There were not so many local jealousies and problems as confronted the uniting churches in the British Isles. On the day of union there was an impressive service of worship in City Road Chapel, which prepared the way for the Uniting Conference at Albert Hall. There were present at that Conference not only the elected representatives of the churches uniting, but as visitors representatives of many churches in the larger Methodist family. The representative of the Federal Council of the Churches of Christ in America was its president, Dr. S. Parkes Cadman, who had been nurtured in a British Methodist Church. As the representative of the Methodist Protestant Church in the United States, there was Dr. John C. Broomfield, its president, afterwards to be a bishop of the United Methodist Church. From the Methodist Episcopal

Church in the United States went Bishop Francis J. McConnell, and I had the privilege of representing the Methodist Episcopal Church, South. There were present also representatives of Methodist Churches from different sections of the British Commonwealth of Nations.

When the vote for union was taken, it was unanimous, and the presidents of the three churches uniting signed the Deed of Union. The great audience of 10,000 people was deeply moved as it sang the *Te Deum*. Through the years since that Union, the British Methodist Church has continued to strengthen its organization, and there is a realization of oneness, though there is also an appreciation of the contribution which each of the uniting churches has made.

Within these years when great unions were consummated, there have been other unions involving smaller groups of Methodists. The American Methodists in Italy have surrendered most of their work to the British Methodist Church. In Germany, where both American and British Methodists began work at about the same time, there is now one German Methodist Church. In France, the British Methodist Churches have become a part of a United Protestant Church. In some of the mission fields of the American Methodist Churches there have been significant developments.

In Mexico, the Methodist Episcopal Church, South, and the Methodist Episcopal Church united their memberships in a Mexican Methodist Church, and gave to that church an autonomous status. The Mexican Church has its separate organization and in its General Conference elects its own bishop. At an earlier date the Boards of Missions of Protestant Churches in the United States had allocated Mexican territory to each denomination, and there is in Mexico a National Council of Churches which seeks to maintain comity agreements and fellowship.

In Japan, the Canadian Methodist Church, the Methodist Episcopal Church of the United States, and the Methodist Episcopal Church, South, had separate missions for many years. These were united in the Methodist Church of Japan, and just before World War II that Church became a part of a larger Protestant movement

36

which resulted in the formation of the United Church of Christ in Japan. There was a similar movement under way in China when the Communists came into control.

At the present time there is a plan under discussion for uniting Protestant Churches in Ceylon and a very ambitious plan for uniting Protestant Churches in North India. It was my privilege to be present at a Central Conference of the Methodist Church in Bangalore, India, in 1953, when this plan for union in North India was being discussed by the Methodists. That Central Conference, after a very interesting discussion of the plan, voted support on all proposals, though it suggested certain changes and amendments. One of the important questions is whether the United Church of North India can still maintain close relations with The Methodist Church in the United States when the Methodist Church of North India becomes a part of the United Church.

Within recent months there has begun a very interesting discussion about the relationship of the British Methodist Church and The Methodist Church in the United States in mission lands where they both have work. The proposal is now being put forward that these churches unite their work. At a recent meeting of missionary leaders of The Methodist Church in the United States, great interest was manifested in a suggestion of Bishop Newell Booth of Africa, that such unions should be sought. He was considering especially situations in Africa. A very significant action was taken by the General Conference of the African Methodist Episcopal Church at Miami in 1956, in the election of a South African negro as bishop of that Church in his home territory. That Church could well enter into the discussions for proposed Methodist union in sections of Africa.

Over the years the Methodists and Presbyterians in New Zealand have discussed a union of those two churches. The Methodist Church seems more interested in such a union at the present time than does the Presbyterian. In Australia various plans of Protestant union have been discussed: one involving all the Protestant Churches; one involving Congregationalists, Methodists, and Presbyterians; and

37

one involving Congregationalists and Methodists. In all of these plans the Methodist Church in Australia has been deeply interested and is more than willing to take the leadership. In the meantime, conversations have taken place between the Anglican Church and the Free Churches in Great Britain.

Since the session of the British Methodist Conference in 1955, the Anglicans and the Methodists have undertaken new conversations, and there is an increasing determination to explore the possibilities of intercommunion as a step toward union. It is reasonable to expect that the results of all of these conversations will bring the Protestant Churches of Great Britain closer together, and with each year the British Council of Churches becomes a stronger body. Some of the most interesting documents in the history of church union have been published as a result of the conversations in Great Britain. In an earlier discussion of Protestant union in Australia there was suggested a formula for supplemental ordination which remains one of the most important contributions in this field. A similar statement was worked out a few years ago in discussions between the Anglican Church and the United Church of Canda. Here are the Preface and the Declaration worked out in the Australian Plan:

Preface

(a) Seeing that the witness of the Church is lamentably weakened by divisions and misunderstanding among Christians, and that responsibility for such human frailty must be shared by all Christian communions, we are led to believe that divergent conceptions of the Ministry have, at least in part, been caused by undue or inadequate emphasis on some functions of the Ministry.

(b) Accordingly, we believe that all who have been called to exercise their ministry, within the limitations of a divided Church, should be enabled to share to the utmost a wider, fuller, and more effectual ministry in a reunited Fellowship.

(c) We are led to the conviction that it is God's Will that this wider and more effectual ministry should be initiated by the mutual laying on of hands with prayer, and with the use of such a formula as shall leave no room for any scruple or doubtfulness.

(d) To effect this purpose, we individually make the following declaration, as a general expression of our convictions, and as a basis of action through which God's Will may be accomplished.

Declaration

(a) I, believing myself to have been called and ordained to a real ministry of the Word and Sacraments in the Church of God, am yet conscious of a desire for that wider, fuller, and more effectual ministry in a reunited fellowship.

(b) I, also believing that it is His Will that all those whom He has thus called should exercise their ministry in One Communion and Fellowship for the building up of His Kingdom, am humbly prepared to receive the mutual laying on of hands with prayer so that all to whom I may lawfully minister within this reunited Fellowship may know without scruple or doubtfulness, that I have been fully ordained and commissioned to preach The Word and to minister The Sacraments.

(c) I, therefore, being persuaded that all power and grace come from Christ, through His Holy Spirit, and that He gave some Apostles, and some Prophets, and some Evangelists, and some Pastors and Teachers, do freely and willingly assent to give and to receive, and to bestow and to share, so far as lies within my power, such further authority as shall seem "good to the Holy Ghost and to us," who in this matter only seek God's glory in the Unity of His Church.

Through its Commission on Church Union, The Methodist Church in the United States has been negotiating for a large Protestant union with churches which recognize each other's orders and ministries. Participating in these discussions from time to time have been the Disciples Church; the Evangelical and Reformed Church; the Presbyterian Church in the United States; the Presbyterian Church in the United States of America; and two Methodist Churches, The Methodist Church in the United States, and the Christian Methodist Church. Since the first meeting of the representatives of these churches was held at Greenwich, Connecticut, in 1950, the plan which has resulted from these discussions is known as The Greenwich

Plan. It seeks to embody Congregational, Episcopal, and Presbyterian polities in the polity of the United Church. It is the first blueprint ever drawn of a United Church with such diverse elements. At the present time that plan is being studied in groups and seminaries of several of the churches concerned. It is also being studied by groups in various American cities which are preparing for a great Conference at Oberlin College in 1957 on "The Nature of the Unity We Seek." The plan is not ready for presentation to any ecclesiastical assembly for approval, but it has aroused much interest in Protestant circles. The heart of that plan is presented in Chapter VII.

The Methodist Church in the United States, through its Commission on Church Union, has been negotiating with the Commission of Approaches to Unity of the Protestant Episcopal Church. These negotiations have been carried on in joint meetings of the two Commissions. It has been my joy to speak to the House of Bishops and also the House of Delegates of the Protestant Episcopal Church in the General Convention. In two successive General Conferences the Chairman of the Episcopal Commission on Approaches to Unity has spoken to the members. For discussion in the meetings of two Commissions there have been presented papers dealing with the episcopacy, the ministry, the polity, the ritual, and the program emphases of the two churches. On the Commission of the Protestant Episcopal Church are those who belong to the High Church group and those who belong to the Low Church group. A beautiful fellowship has developed, and there have come deep understandings both of agreements and differences.

At a meeting of the Executive Committee of the World Methodist Council at Evanston in 1954, it was decided that all plans involving a Methodist Church in any land should be presented for discussion to this Executive Committee. While the Executive Committee has no such authority as the Lambeth Conference in the Anglican Church, it has seemed that all members of the Methodist family should be apprised of discussions of union entered into by any member of that family in any land. That is essential as we seek to preserve the unity among Methodists throughout the world. That decision grew out of a discussion of union movements in many lands.

It seems to some Methodist leaders that union movements within a land may lead to a creation of national churches, and that enthusiasm for national churches would break the fellowship within the world organization of Methodism. On the other hand, there are Methodist leaders who feel that any united church in any land can continue to maintain its fellowship with the larger denominational family, just as the United Church of Canada maintains its fellowship with the World Methodist Council. There is no more important question raised within the World Church today than this particular question. The World Council of Churches has in its membership individual churches or denominations. Is the unity within the larger Methodist family broken when one branch of that family unites with other denominations in any country? Must we Methodists favor the one approach or the other? Is it possible to maintain both approaches, to favor Protestant union within the land and at the same time seek to promote a world denominational organization?

We are living in a world with many political divisions in which we are definitely conscious of national and racial differences. Would Methodism best fulfill its mission to the world if it sought to transcend these differences in the building of world fellowship? If this be the case, are we approaching the time when we ought to be thinking of one World Methodist Church? At the Oxford Conference in 1951, Bishop J. W. E. Sommer of Germany argued strongly that we must begin to think about such a world church. If we plan for that, we must consider its relationship to the World Council of Churches.

At one time I had the temerity to suggest that the Assembly of the World Council of Churches should be made up of two groups, just as in many governments there are two legislative bodies. In Great Britain there are the House of Commons and the House of

Lords. In the United States there are the House of Representatives and the Senate. The World fellowships or organizations could select representatives for one group and the individual denominations could select representatives for the other group in the Assembly of the World Council. This might not be the best of solutions, but its purpose would be to hold all the unions we are able to establish.

For a long time the history of the Christian Church was marked by divisions and further divisions. Within our generation another process has set in, a process of union and unions. The Methodist Church is true to its genius and true to its history when it supports movements for co-operation and movements for union. Not only in theory but in practice, it desires to meet its responsibility in the realization of One Church, as there is One Lord.

CHAPTER IV

AIDS TO ECUMENICITY

I. Travel

In RECENT YEARS there have been increasing contacts between various sections of the Methodist world. The bishops of The Methodist Church in the United States have made frequent visits to the mission fields of that church. In fact, every bishop is required to make a trip to some mission field at least once during a quadrennium. These journeys have taken our American leaders to Asia, Africa, Europe, and South America. While visiting mission stations in the various continents, these bishops have had an opportunity to establish contacts with other Methodists and with Christians of other denominations.

It has been the plan of the World Council of Churches to arrange meetings of the Central Committee in different sections of the world. These meetings have taken officials of that body to Australia, India, and to different nations of Europe. Meetings are planned for Hungary and Ceylon. In line with such meetings, it has been the purpose of the world Methodist Council to hold the regular sessions of the Executive Committee in different countries. There has been an increasing interchange of Methodist leaders within the Methodist family. Perhaps the most interesting assemblies, outside the regular meetings of the World Methodist Council, have been those held in connection with the First Assembly of the World Council of Churches at Amsterdam and the Second Assembly of the World Council at Evanston. At the former some three hundred Methodists were present and at the latter approximately five hundred, coming from a score or more of Methodist Churches. These Assemblies were presided over by the President of the World Methodist Council, and words of greeting were brought from all over the world. Such Assemblies have brought an acquaintance among Methodist leaders which has not been known before. These many contacts in travel have done more than bring widely separated Methodists together. They have brought a new sense of the world-wide character of Methodism.

II. The Exchange of Preachers

Ever since the Springfield Conference of 1947 we have had a program of exchanging preachers, particularly between Great Britain and the United States. The Chairman of the British Committee is the Reverend A. Stanley Leyland, and the Chairman of the American Committee is Dr. Karl Quimby. These men and their committees have rendered a great service to world Methodism. At the Oxford Conference of 1951, there was a luncheon at Christ Church at which a score of Methodist preachers told of their experiences in these exchanges. It was one of the inspiring hours of the Oxford Conference. These men have been ambassadors of good will not only for their churches but for their nations. Each summer six or seven men have gone from the United States to Great Britain and six or seven have come from Great Britain to the United States. We have had two exchanges with Austria and one with Germany. In recent months an exchange has been worked out be-between the Caribbean Area of British Methodism and Methodist ministers in Florida. For the first time it has been possible to bring understandings between the United States and the Islands of the West Indies. In addition to the students who go from time to time from Australia, New Zealand, and other sections of the British Commonwealth to study in Great Britain, there has been an increasing number of students in American universities and theological schools from Australasia.

Under a program of the Board of Missions of The Methodist Church in the United States, Crusade Scholars have come to study in the United States from each of the mission fields of the American church. There have been other agencies than those of the church which have promoted this exchange of students. It is the hope of the World Methodist Council that it may be possible to bring teachers in schools of theology from one country to another. At least three American Methodist seminaries have had in recent years teachers from British seminaries, and a plan is under way which will bring teachers from Australia and New Zealand to the United States.

The Board of Evangelism of the American Church has sent missioners on evangelistic missions from the United States to half a dozen foreign lands, and there is contemplated now a mission to Australia and New Zealand. This same Board has brought to the United States for a year Dr. Alan Walker who was the leader of the "Mission to the Nation" in Australia.

III. The Upper Room

Helping to bring about an eventual world-wide renewal of spiritual strength through providing a simple, easily followed guide for devotions is the romance of *The Upper Room.*

Published in 27 languages and in Braille, the little periodical is helping more than ten million people turn to God daily in family and private devotions. Since its inception in 1935, *The Upper Room* has reached every continent and most of the islands of the seas. *The Upper Room* meets a very definite need in a very definite way. However, it offers no new magic formula. The family altar and daily devotions are as old as mankind. Anyone may talk with God at any time. He may read his Bible and meditate whenever he wishes. God's availability to the individual without intervention of any kind is basic in Protestant belief.

But *The Upper Room* does make it simple and easy to enjoy daily devotions. Each day's devotion is made up of a suggested Bible reading, a scripture text, a brief meditation, a prayer, and a thought for the day. The individual or family may expand and build upon these basic devotional aids.

From the very beginning of the ministry of *The Upper Room,* it became evident that this formula effectively meets a need. Born in the spring of 1935 while the United States sought a cure for the economic ills that beset it, *The Upper Room* met with immediate acceptance. It was hardly an auspicious time to start any new project. Yet from its very inception, this booklet seemed destined to affect the world profoundly. As the years pass, it becomes more and more apparent that the early promise is being fulfilled. The publication, launched with high purpose in a perilous economic era, was born in prayer and faith.

It was readily admitted at that time that the average man inside the church and without did not read his Bible and that he seldom was able to lead in prayer, even in the privacy of his own home. What was to be done about this vacuum in American life caused by the passing of the family altar and regular individual devotions? A secretary of the Board of Missions of the then Methodist Episcopal Church, South, Dr. Grover C. Emmons, thought he knew. Dr. Emmons under the direction of the Evangelism Committee of the Board of Missions launched *The Upper Room* in 1935 and was its editor for nine years. Following the death of Dr. Emmons in April, 1944, Dr. Roy H. Short of Louisville, Kentucky, was chosen as editor-in-chief. In 1948 Dr. Short became a bishop of The Methodist Church. Dr. J. Manning Potts of Virginia was chosen as the third editor. Dr. Potts had been a friend of Dr. Emmons and had served on the Board of Evangelism and The Upper Room Committee, which determines the policy of the publication. Working with the editor are more than one hundred and twenty-five people who daily handle *The Upper Room*. As for the meditations, two months are spent in gathering and editing material for each issue. Then, seven months before distribution date, the copy must go to the printer. Otherwise it would be impossible to meet the needs of the ten million people it guides in daily devotions in all parts of the world.

There seems to be no limit to the effective ministry of *The Upper Room*. As it grows in usefulness, meeting the spiritual needs of individuals and families, it is winning people to Christ. It is building happy lives by helping persons to be at home with God in their homes. From the home, the influence of *The Upper Room* spreads into the community, from the community to the nation, and from the nation out across the world, helping to bring about an eventual world-wide renewal of spiritual strength.

"Go ye into all the world, and preach the gospel to every creature." The Master's injunction to His disciples is being followed faithfully by the world's most widely used devotional guide. The part it can play in bringing to fruition the dream of a Christian world is a task and a challenge accepted with deep humility by the men and women who serve on the staff of The Upper Room.

Almost from its beginning, *The Upper Room* has been published in other languages. It is now printed in thirty-two editions, in twenty-six languages other than English and Braille. The idea of the evangelistic and missionary importance of a devotional guide was inherent in the vision of what *The Upper Room* might become.

As examples, let us look at a brief history of two of these twenty-six other-language editions. One of the earlier of the other-language editions is the Korean, which was first published in Seoul in the fall of 1938. The Korean edition was published regularly until the beginning of World War II, when it had to be discontinued. In 1948 plans were made to resume publication. Again it was started in Seoul. When Seoul was evacuated during the Korean War, publication headquarters were moved to Japan. When the North Koreans were driven out of Seoul, the editors returned; and it was published in Seoul once more. When the editors were driven out of Seoul the second time, once again they planned to publish it in Japan, but were able to print it in Pusan, Korea. With the ending of hostilities, the edition was again published in Seoul, which is its present headquarters. The Korean edition has labored under greater difficulties than any other of the editions of *The Upper Room*.

The Chinese edition, first published in 1947, in Shanghai, China, has a most interesting history. While the conflict has been going on between the Reds and Nationalists in China, it has been difficult to produce a Chinese edition. Due to this conflict, publication of the edition was ceased for awhile. Publication was resumed early in 1954 with headquarters in Hong Kong. Considering what has been happening in China, the history of the Chinese edition is phenomenal.

In 1944 another edition in English was begun. Due to the war situation, it was thought wise to produce a pocket edition, especially for the men and women in the armed forces. This edition was very popular during the war, and since the war has grown in popularity among civilians, especially youth. It is now called the Air Mail edition.

The Upper Room is happy in its outreach, its transcendence of race and nationality. With two exceptions the other-language editions are subsidized through contributions by the readers of *The Upper Room*. It is only through contributions that the missionary and evangelistic work of *The Upper Room* can be carried on.

There are other publications which aid the Ecumenical Movement, though there is none which quite so truly meets the challenge to spread ecumenicity as *The Upper Room*. Perhaps the best known of other publications is *The World Parish* which does for World Methodism what the *Ecumenical Review* does for the World Council of Churches. This has been under the editorship of Dr. Elmer T. Clark from the beginning of its publication and goes to all the representatives of the World Methodist Council. Its circulation is not very large. There is no other religious publication with such a circulation as *The Upper Room*.

The circulation of *The Upper Room* for the last twelve months has been 18,419,132. This means an average of 3,069,855 paid circulation per issue. This is an increase of 627,941 copies over the previous year, or an average increase of 104,657 per issue. It is interesting to note that every issue but one set a new record in paid circulation.

Some time ago *The Upper Room* was described as ecumenicity at the grass roots. *The Upper Room* is just that. It is world-wide, international, interdenominational, and interracial. Six of the editions are in English; and three of the English editions are published out-side the United States, one in Scotland, another in India, and the third in Australia. Only four of the thirty-two editions are published in the United States and only three of these in Nashville. Every working day more than 75,000 copies of *The Upper Room* go out of the Shipping Department at 1908 Grand Avenue, Nashville. They go to all the states of the Union and to more than one hundred countries. Recently, for the first time in its history, the circulation of *The Upper Room* through the Nashville post office passed 3,000,000 copies of one issue.

The Upper Room is used by churches of most of the denominations in America. In Canada *The Upper Room* has the sponsorship of the United Church of Canada through its Board of Evangelism and Social Service, but its use in Canada is not confined to the United Church. It has a wide circulation in the Baptist churches. In fact, many of the largest orders for *The Upper Room* are from Baptist churches in Canada.

The Hungarian edition of *The Upper Room* is published in Canada and is sponsored by the Executive Committee of the Presbyterian Church. This edition circulates mainly among refugees, but copies go out to many parts of the world.

The Spanish edition, which is published in Nashville, Tennessee, circulates chiefly in the United States, Central America, South America, and the West Indies. The circulation is quite large in some of the cities of the United States. It has a wide circulation in Cuba where it is used by several denominations.

The only edition published in South America is the edition sponsored by the Methodist Church of Brazil and the Federal Council of Churches in that land. It is the Portuguese edition, and it is sent from Sao Paulo to other Portuguese countries such as Angola, Portuguese East Africa, and Portugal itself.

In Europe there are seven editions of *The Upper Room*. They are published by several different agencies. The Norwegian edition is published in Oslo by the Methodist Church of Norway. The

Swedish edition is published in Stockholm by the Methodist Church of Sweden. The Finnish edition is published in Helsinki by the Lutheran Church. The Russian edition is translated in Finland and published in Gothenburg by the Interdenominational Russian Slavic Society. It ministers largely to refugees scattered in many places. The British Isles edition is published in Stirling, Scotland, by the Stirling Tract Society, and its leaders are Baptists.

There is the Italian edition published in Rome by the British Methodist Church. The Greek edition in Athens is published by the Evangelical Church of Greece, which church is a member of the World Reformed Alliance.

There are four editions published in the Middle East and the Near East. The Turkish edition is published in Istanbul under the sponsorship of the American Board (Congregational Christian). The Armenian and Arabic editions are published in Beirut, Lebanon, both sponsored by the Christian Endeavor Society. The Armenian edition is published in the Evangelical Church Press, and the Arabic edition is published in the Presbyterian Publishing House. In Iran the Persian edition is published by the Presbyterian Mission.

In the Orient there are 17 editions of *The Upper Room*. In India there are five, the Gujarati edition is published by the Church of the Brethren Press in Gujarat, India. The Hindi edition and the English edition in India are published by the Methodist Publishing House in Lucknow. The Telugu edition is sponsored by the Hyderabad Christian Council and published in the Lutheran Publishing House. The Tamil edition is published by the American Board (Congregational Christian). The Indian editions have other additional sponsorships. The Urdu edition is published in Lahore, Pakistan, sponsored by the West Pakistan Christian Council, with Canon Chandu Ray of the Church of England as editor.

The Thai edition is published in Bangkok by the Presbyterian Church. The Chinese edition is published in Hong Kong by the Methodist Church. The Japanese edition is published in Tokyo by the United Church of Japan, and the Korean edition is published in Seoul by the Methodist Church of Korea.

There are three editions in the Philippines. Two of these, the Ilocano and Tagalog, are published by the Methodist Church of the Philippines. The Cebuano is published jointly by the Methodist Church and the United Church of the Philippines. The Australasian edition is published by the Methodist Church of Australasia and has a circulation in New Zealand and the isles of the Pacific.

The newest edition of *The Upper Room* is the French edition which was started last January in Haiti. It is sponsored by the British Methodist Church in Haiti.

Two new editions are to be published soon: Talking Book and the Burmese. Talking Book is sponsored by the men of the Methodist Church of London, Kentucky, and has the full co-operation of the John Milton Society, interdenominational organization publishing religious literature for the blind. The Burmese is to be published by the Christian Literature Committee of Burma. Both are due January 1, and will bring the number of editions of *The Upper Room* to thirty-four.

It is seen by this description that *The Upper Room* is published in many different countries and on all continents except the continent of Africa. However, *The Upper Room* has a large circulation in Africa.

From time to time there are questions as to the interracial flavor of *The Upper Room*. Representatives from every race have contributed to the pages of *The Upper Room*. Every mail brings meditations voluntarily contributed from many parts of the world. They come from many different people and many different cultural groups. It is the policy of The Upper Room to continuously stress its interracial character. Unless one knows the writer of the particular day's meditation, he will not know the color of the person's skin who wrote the meditation. In special issues of *The Upper Room*, such as the Lay Witness Number and the Christian Fellowship Number, people of every station in life are represented.

The ecumenical flavor of *The Upper Room* at the grass roots is seen in its readers, its writers, and its outreach.

IV. Other Aids

At the Ninth World Methodist Conference there will be used a small hymnal, with hymns and tunes known on both sides of the Atlantic. Does this indicate that we may have before many years one Methodist Hymnal used around the world? Long before Methodist Union in the United States, a generation before it came, there was published a Methodist Hymnal for use in the larger and separated Methodist Churches. It served to draw Methodists closer together, and was a factor in the promotion of Union. Perhaps a common hymnal for use in all the Methodist Churches of the world may serve to promote a United Methodist Church of the World.

The visit of an increasing number of Methodists to Wesley's City Road Chapel and the New Room in Bristol brings to them a realization of their great heritage, and the Wesleyan tradition becomes a unifying inspiration to Methodists of many lands. I was present at a recent Sunday service in City Road Chapel when there were representatives of thirteen lands in the congregation.

CHAPTER V

METHODISM DEEPENS ITS WORLD FELLOWSHIP IN THE WEST INDIES, AUSTRALIA, AND NEW ZEALAND

I. Hands Across the Caribbean

THE ISLAND of Antigua is in the Leeward Group of the West Indies and lies far to the east off the coast of Florida. At the capital city of St. Johns in October, 1954, the Provincial Council of the Caribbean Area was held. Dr. Elmer T. Clark, Dr. J. Manning Potts, and I arrived at St. Johns by Pan American plane on Sunday, October 17th. We were met by the Minister of the Methodist Church in St. Johns and by our host, the Honorable J. Moody-Stuart. Our host was born in Scotland, and his wife is the third generation of her family on the Island of Antigua. They are in charge of large sugar plantations which are the main sources of revenue. On the island are thirty-five thousand people, with only five hundred white people. The others are descendants of the slaves of early days.

Against this economic-social background we recall the beginnings of Methodism in the West Indies. It was in 1760 that a sugar planter by the name of Nathaniel Gilbert went to England. There he heard John Wesley preach and was converted in one of his meetings. Returning to the island, he began to preach to his slaves. At about the same time a Methodist immigrant came to Antigua, a ship's carpenter by the name of Baxter. He worked at the dockyards, and it was here that the fleet of Lord Nelson was prepared for the Battle of Trafalgar. Here also ships were made ready for their conflicts with Dutch, French, and Spanish fleets. In some way Baxter went to the Christmas Conference of 1784 when the Methodist

Church was organized in the new American nation. At that Conference he received ordination and was appointed to Antigua. The American preacher who was appointed with him died before he could sail, and Baxter returned alone to carry on Methodist work on Antigua. If the American preacher had lived, the Methodism of the West Indies might have been more closely related to American Methodism.

It was at the holiday season of 1785-1786 that Thomas Coke came to Antigua with three Methodist preachers from England. It is interesting to note that the founder of Methodism in the West Indies is the same man whom Mr. Wesley sent to organize the Methodist Church in the United States. In spite of the fact that the two Methodisms had the same leader in the beginning, there has been no contact in the hundred and seventy years of history. American Methodism is found on the Island of Cuba and on the Island of Puerto Rico. Stopping over for a day with our Methodists in Puerto Rico, we found that they know nothing about Methodism in the British West Indies. We were afterwards to learn that the Methodists on the other islands know nothing about Methodism in Cuba and Puerto Rico. Certainly we were the first Americans in nearly two hundred years who ever paid an official visit to these Methodists who live so near to our country. We went as representatives of the World Methodist Council and not as representatives of American Methodism.

Some months ago we decided in the World Methodist Council to relate Methodism in the West Indies to our American office and Methodism on the continent of Europe, which is mainly American in origin, to the British office. In this way we are bringing about understanding and deepening fellowship. We were received most graciously by the Provincial Council. There were delegates present from Jamaica, Trinidad, Haiti, St. Croix, Barbadoes, British Guiana, British Honduras, Panama, the Bahamas, and several other small islands. The British secretary in charge of work in the West Indies, from the Mission House in London, was present through the sessions. He is the Reverend Wilfred Easton who was at Evanston for the Executive Committee of the World Methodist Council and for the World Council of Churches.

Each night there was a public meeting; and the church, which seats six hundred to seven hundred people, was crowded. I preached on Sunday night, Dr. Clark spoke on Monday night, and Dr. Potts spoke on Tuesday night. We were all impressed by the fine spirit of worship and the excellent singing, both of the large choir and the congregation. Each morning and afternoon there were sessions of the Council, and each of the Americans spoke at these business meetings, seeking to relate West Indian Methodism more closely to the World Methodist Council. There we learned to place a very high estimate on the quality of leadership which Methodism has in the Caribbean Area. This was true of those who had come out from England as well as of the native leaders. One of the real problems is to train more adequately a larger native leadership.

As I look back on the experiences of those inspiring days in Antigua, I carry with me these impressions: (1) Methodism is a vigorous, religious movement in the West Indies, as it has been from the beginning. In the early years there was much persecution which came both from the government and the Established Church. Men were thrown in prison and their lives were threatened because the slaves were the ones to whom the early Methodists preached. These Methodist leaders were looked upon as creators of strife and wrong attitudes among the slaves. The opposition arose out of a desire to maintain the economic and social status quo. As the years have passed Methodism has not only been a factor in the liberation of slaves, but in the improvement of conditions among the masses of people. (2) There are now at least two hundred and fifty thousand Methodists in the West Indies, though this figure would include some who call themselves Methodists but are actually not communicant members of the Church. If more money were available for the building of churches, more congregations could easily be established. Among the members of the Methodist Church are many who hold very high positions in economic and political circles. The Governor of Jamaica, sent out from England, is a Methodist and the son of a very distinguished British layman. As is true everywhere, Methodism exerts an influence beyond its proportionate numerical strength. (3) There is a deep spiritual quality in the religious life of these people in the West Indies. That is apparent in every service of worship. Of course, there is immorality where people live in poverty and are crowded together, but the young people in our Methodist churches are striving valiantly to lead decent lives and to keep high moral standards. (4) An examination of the agenda reveals the fact that organizational problems are the same as in other sections of the Methodist world. It is likewise apparent that Methodist zeal for evangelism and Methodist preaching of the gospel of hope in a world of despair are as much in the thinking of the Methodists of the West Indies as in the thinking of those in other parts of the world.

It is my earnest hope that the Methodists of the United States will come to know these Methodists in the West Indies. Many of our rich families have found the Island of Antigua a place of rest and recreation. On the east end is a magnificent American club, and there can be found a score of luxurious winter homes erected by men of prominence and wealth in our American cities. Although some of our people have found a playground for the winter months, our Methodist people should think of those islands as the homelands of some of the most devout Methodists in the world.

In February of 1955 Mrs. Holt and I went to Nassau for a visit with the Methodists of the Bahamas. We were entertained by prominent Methodist laymen, one of whom is the leader of the Lower House and the other the leader of the Upper House in the legislative assembly. It was my privilege to preach in three of our churches in Nassau and to meet our Methodist leaders at tea in the college Methodists maintain.

We can never forget the fact that on Monday, as we went to shops along the principal business street, some person in every shop greeted us as though we were old friends. These persons had been to one or another of the Methodist churches the day before. We concluded that business in Nassau is in the hands of the Methodists. Never have we received any finer expressions of appreciation.

As a result of the visit we had the first exchange of preachers between the Bahamas and the American mainland in the summer of 1955. One of the teachers at the college came to the First Methodist Church in Jacksonville Beach, Florida, and the pastor of that church went to Nassau. Each of them had a wonderful experience, and this exchange will continue, thanks to the co-operation of Mr. Easton and the London Mission House.

Then in August of 1955, as we flew home from South America, Mrs. Holt and I stopped in Kingston, Jamaica, as the guests of the Reverend and Mrs. W. H. Totty. It was a kind of return visit because the Jamaica superintendent had been on an extended speaking engagement in the United States earlier in the summer. Never will I forget the service on Sunday morning at Coke Church. Mr. Totty had charge of the service. The Governor, the Honorable Hugh Foot, read the lessons in the service, and I preached. Since I had known the Rt. Honorable Isaac Foot for many years, it was a great joy to have his son participate in the service of the church where he is a regular attendant. His warm letter of appreciation concerning my sermon I will treasure always.

Recently the editor of American Methodism's devotional magazine, *The Upper Room*, went to Haiti and arranged for the publication of a French edition of that periodical. It was possible for Dr. J. Manning Potts to make that arrangement because British Methodism was established there, and Mr. H. O. McConnell had received some financial help from America in the building of his new church after the destructive hurricane. Letters bring people together across the miles, but personal visits are worth more than thousands of letters in bringing Methodists to a realization of the fact that they are one people around the world.

II. A Visit to the Methodists of Australia and New Zealand

Twenty years ago I went to Australia when I was President of the Federal Council of Churches of Christ in America. That visit took me to Brisbane, Sydney, Canberra, Melbourne, and Adelaide. I gave a series of lectures in Adelaide at the Congregational College; preached at Scots Church in Melbourne, the Presbyterian Cathedral Church; addressed a Council of Churches meeting in Sydney; and was present as a fraternal delegate at the Centennial General Conference of the Methodist Church. Since becoming president of the World Methodist Council, I had to cancel my engagements, but during the Lenten Season of 1955 I was able to make my long anticipated trip. I was accompanied by the editor of *The Upper Room*, Dr. J. Manning Potts. That journal, which has so great a value in our Ecumenical Movement, has a wide circulation in Australia. We flew from San Francisco to Auckland via Honolulu and the Fiji Islands.

It has been 75 years since The Methodist Church of the United States established work in the Hawaiian Islands. In the spring of 1955 over one hundred Methodists came from the mainland to help celebrate the anniversary. For the first time the Methodist work in the Hawaiian Islands is under the superintendency of a native son of Honolulu, the able Japanese Methodist leader, Harry Komuro. The First Methodist Church in Honolulu is interracial, as are churches on the Island of Oahu and other islands. In addition, in Honolulu there are Chinese, Hawaiian, Japanese, and Korean Methodist Churches. On one Sunday I preached in English at the Japanese Methodist Church and participated in a broadcast of the Council of Churches. On another Sunday I preached in the Central Union Church, established by the Congregationalists. It is interracial and is by far the strongest Protestant Church in Honolulu.

Arriving in Auckland, we were met by one of the Home Mission Secretaries of the New Zealand Church. He and the Chief Secretary had arranged an itinerary for us. We had expressed a desire to see as many of our ministers as possible, and in meetings in seven centers we met about two hundred of our two hundred and twenty-five ministers. The centers visited were, in addition to Auckland, Rotorua, Wellington, Nelson, Christchurch, Dunedin, and Invercargill. Everywhere we had a most cordial welcome, and I am sure that no foreign visitors ever had the privilege of meeting so large a proportion of the Methodist ministers of New Zealand. We went from the top of the North Island to the bottom of the South Island. While the Church of England and the Presbyterian Church are stronger than the Methodist Church, we found our church active and vigorous. Within recent years New Zealand Methodist leaders have made visits to both Great Britain and the United States, but they feel that they are a long way from other Methodisms. The purpose of my visit was to make the Methodists in those interesting islands conscious of their importance in the Methodist family and of their relationship to it.

The two Sundays I spent in the islands were given to services in Auckland and Christchurch. At the morning hour in each of those cities I preached in a church in a residential area and at the evening hour in a downtown or central mission church. There were excellent congregations, and at every service I met people who had contacts with Methodism in Great Britain or in the United States. Another interesting experience came in the Auckland churches. At the morning service were ten or twelve students of the university who had come from the Tongan Islands, and at the evening service there were at least twenty students from Samoa. The influence of New Zealand Methodism is felt in other islands. The principal of the Theological College in Auckland is president of the International Historical Society of the World Methodist Council, and one of the professors had just returned home from a period of study in the United States. There were delightful visits with the President of the Conference at Nelson and a former President at Christchurch who led the delegation to the Springfield World Conference in 1947, with the Chairmen of Districts, with the Editor of the *Methodist Times* and the Secretary of the Conference, with the pastors of the churches where I preached, and with scores of preachers in fellowship gatherings. Never can I forget the long drive through the scenic areas of the South Island, when one of the pastors gave me glimpses of some of the most magnificent mountain scenery in the world. On the wall of my study hangs a picture of one of those glorious mountains to remind me of a country and a people I was privileged to know so well during my weeks of travel.

Flying from Christchurch to Sydney in a few hours, I began my visit to the Methodists of Australia. Dr. Potts and I were together through most of the Australian visit, but there were times when we separated in order to reach more Methodist centers. In Brisbane we both spoke at a Sunday afternoon meeting of Methodists of the Brisbane Area, but at the morning and evening services we were in different churches. I went on a very rainy Sunday night to the church of the President of the Queensland Conference.

Then we went to Adelaide where we visited the colleges for girls and for boys, spoke at a great Methodist meeting in Pirie Street Church, were the guests of the President of the South Australia Conference at his college, saw the Old Folks Home and the Broadcasting Station of our Central Mission, called on some of the retired ministers, and drove scores of miles along the sea and in the hills.

Going to Sydney, we were given a Civic Reception by the Lord Mayor and welcomed in an Interdenominational Service at the Anglican Cathedral, presided over by the Primate of the Anglican Church, the Archbishop of Sydney. Dr. Potts and I preached at lovely suburban churches on Sunday morning, and I had the privilege of preaching Sunday night to the great congregation at the important Methodist center in the heart of the city. Never can I forget that experience or the contacts with the Theological College and Wesley College, and one of the stimulating meetings was that of the ministers of New South Wales Methodism on a Monday, presided over by the President of the New South Wales Conference. In Sydney Dr. Potts stayed at the Theological College, and at the Ladies College there I was the guest of the President General of

Australasian Methodism. For a day of rest and recreation, we had a long automobile trip with Methodist friends to the Blue Mountains.

Departing for Melbourne, Dr. Potts spoke on Good Friday at our Central Mission, while I flew two thousand miles to Perth for Good Friday services and a meeting with the ministers of Western Australia. Never have I seen such a throng of people at a Good Friday evening service as I saw at Perth, and it is not often that visitors to Australia go to that lovely city. Then I returned to Melbourne for Easter Sunday and two great services, one the Pleasant Sunday Afternoon whose broadcast is heard by three million people, and the other on Easter Sunday evening.

While Dr. Potts flew to Perth for Easter Sunday and on to Singapore, I returned to Sydney. In Melbourne the President of the Victoria Conference gave a reception for us and brought together the ministers of the Area for an afternoon meeting and tea.

Never can I forget visits at our Theological College with the Principal and with one of the professors. The latter took me on a long drive into the mountains. I called at the Methodist Hospital and also at the Methodist Ladies College, though the Principal at the college was leaving on a long trip to Great Britain. The leaders of Australian Methodism are among the ablest in the Methodist World.

On my return to Sydney, I was the guest of the Minister of Leichhardt Mission, who once had been a pastor in the United States; and we went with the President General to Canberra and to a service in our National Church. I met there government officials who are Methodists and called to see the American Ambassador and his wife. American Methodism has made a generous gift for the building of the National Church in Canberra, and as a reminder of my visit I presented to that Church a pulpit Bible. Such a Bible I gave also to the Leichhardt Mission in Sydney.

Then came the long flight from Sydney to Seattle, a distance of 8,000 miles across the Pacific, with stops in the Fiji Islands and at Honolulu. It was a journey of thirty thousand miles by air, and it took me to the capitals of all the Australian States except Tasmania and brought me an acquaintance with several hundred of our Methodist ministers in the Conferences of Australia.

As I look back over the visit to the Methodists of Australia and New Zealand, these reflections come to mind:

(a) In Australia the communicant membership is about 350,000, but in a government census over 800,000 people called themselves Methodists. Likewise in New Zealand the strength of the church is far greater than the communicant membership would show. In South Australia Methodism is stronger than in either of the other states, and probably half of the people would register as Methodists, the actual membership being 27 per cent of the population.

(b) Methodism has excellent schools in Australia for both boys and girls, and the college buildings are imposing. At four centers in Australia, and in New Zealand, Methodist Theological Colleges are preparing men for the ministry, with scholarly teachers and comprehensive courses of study. The problems are those of a new country and are very similar to those faced by American Methodists. The roots of both intellectual life and spiritual life go down into British soil. There is no place in the world where one becomes more deeply conscious of the value of a world-wide Methodist fellowship than in the countries "down under." In the church programs Methodists in Australia and America can plan together because they face the same environments, but Australia and New Zealand still draw their inspiration and spiritual fervor from the Methodism of Great Britain.

(c) The missionary zeal of our Methodists in the South Pacific is inspiring. New Zealand is doing a fine piece of missionary work in the South Pacific. Australian Methodism has done almost a miraculous thing in the conversion of the Fijians. Stopping for dinner at the airport in Fiji, I asked the boy who waited on our table in the dining room, "Are you a Methodist?" On receiving an affirmative answer, I asked the others. They were all Methodists. It was not surprising because ninety per cent of the Fijians are Methodists. That is the densest Methodist population in the world.

To the Methodists in Australia and New Zealand we were able to carry the assurance, "You are a part of a very great Methodist Church." From the Methodists in that part of the world we can carry an inspiration and a zeal that will enrich the spiritual life of Methodists everywhere. To them we take much but from them we also receive much.

We heard on every hand fine reports of the "Mission to the Nation" led by Alan Walker. Through him and his associates I was given the privilege of broadcasting in several of the important religious service hours. Now Alan Walker is making a great impression in our American Methodist Church during the year 1956, which he is spending in the United States.

Other denominations were most cordial in their welcome. The Archbishop of Sydney, the Primate of the Church of England in Australia, and the Archbishop of Melbourne have long been my personal friends, and it was a deep satisfaction to have fellowship with them. The Archbishop of Sydney arranged in his Cathedral a Protestant welcome for Dr. Potts and me, and the representatives of the Protestant churches of Sydney participated. In Australia, as elsewhere, Methodism has an honored place in the larger Christian family.

CHAPTER VI

METHODISM DEEPENS ITS WORLD FELLOWSHIP IN LATIN AMERICA AND ASIA

I. Methodism in Latin America

AFTER the unification of American Methodism it was decided that a bishop in the homeland should be made Official Visitor to some mission field to act as a contact. My episcopal residence being in Dallas, Texas, at the time, I was named Official Visitor to Latin America. In the years from 1940 to 1948 I went to Mexico two or three times a year, to Central America once every year, and to South America every four years. I came to know the Methodism of Latin America almost as well as the area for which I was the administrative bishop, and in those eight years American Methodism invested more money in Latin America than for a generation before.

The General Conference of the Brazil Methodist Church met in Rio de Janeiro in July, 1955, and I went not only as the officially designated representative of the Council of Bishops of the American Church but also as President of the World Methodist Council. Mrs. Holt and I flew from Paris to Lisbon, to Dakar, to Recife, and on to Rio de Janeiro. The sessions of the Conference were held at Bennett College, Methodism's fine school for girls in the capital city. It was seventy-five years ago that the first Methodist missionaries from the United States arrived in Brazil, and in two generations the church has developed able native leadership. One recognized this ability in the debate and discussions at Conference. The Church in Brazil now has a membership of forty-six thousand. The Roman Catholic Eucharistic Congress was held in Rio de Janeiro at the same time, and the throngs attending its sessions made one realize that Methodists are a decidedly minority group.

The Roman Catholic Church insists that South America is a Christian continent and that there should be no Protestant missionaries, but Roman Catholic authorities state that the Church has in South America only a fraction of the priests needed for an adequate ministry. The President of a great Catholic College in the United States, after a thorough study of the religious situation in South America, has written a book in which he asserts that the Church would have to have forty thousand more priests than it has in South America to give to the people such a ministry as is given to the Roman Catholic population of the United States. The ministry of Protestant missionaries is not an attempt to proselyte Catholics so much as an effort to convert those who have no religious allegiance or interest. Many of the ablest business and political leaders in any South American country have broken with the church and are secularists or agnostics, never attending church or receiving Communion. The Protestant church has hoped for years to win these leaders, but they know nothing of Protestant tradition in their experience. Protestantism must develop its own leadership in the community. That it is beginning to do.

The Methodist Church has about thirty thousand boys and girls in its schools in South America, and in many places the Methodist school is easily the outstanding educational institution, surpassing those of the State and the Roman Catholic Church. By way of illustration, the finest college for women in Chile, both in equipment and in curriculum, is Santiago College. The principal of that college received recently the highest decoration the Chilean government confers though she is a Protestant missionary in a Roman Catholic country.

During World War II, I was in Bolivia. The American Church has in that state two schools of influence, one in La Paz and one in Cochabamba. The Board of Missions had decided that it must close the school in La Paz because of reduced income. The American Ambassador invited me to see him and said, "You cannot close this school. If the Methodist Church cannot maintain it, then the

American Government must find a way to do it." At the time it was uncertain whether Bolivia would side with Nazi Germany or with the United States.

In Cochabamba we had to erect a new building; so we called together a group of leading citizens to inquire of them as to the value of the school to the community. The manager of the Rubber Development Corporation, created to get rubber from Bolivia and Brazil after the Japanese shut off the supply from Malaya, said, "The American Government has to have rubber if it wins the war and this is the only place to get it. I am getting it, but I could not have organized our company if it had not been for the two Methodist schools in Bolivia. Ninety-five per cent of our employees are graduates or former students of these two Methodist schools in Bolivia."

Conference after Conference in the United States has been investing missionary funds in the churches and schools of South America—the Philadelphia Conference has put seventy-five thousand dollars into a school building in Peru, the Michigan Conferences have invested a like sum in churches in Chile, and the St. Louis Conference will spend one hundred thousand dollars in erecting church buildings in Peru. The church in Brazil is stronger than in any other section, and the dozen fine schools Methodism has established in that land alone will insure further development. For the Portuguese-speaking population of Brazil and the training of preachers, there is an excellent Seminary at Sao Paulo; and in the same city the Methodist Church has its printing house. For Spanish-speaking South America the Theological Seminary is at Buenos Aires. Its buildings would compare well with those in other sections of the Methodist world, and the faculty is very able. The seminary is supported largely by the Methodist Church, but it is a Union Seminary. One member of the faculty is from the Waldensian Church, there are at least fifteen hundred Waldensians in Uruguay; one member of the faculty is a Presbyterian; one member is from the Disciples of Christ; the others are Methodists. The Methodist Church has work in Brazil, Uruguay, Argentina, Chile, Peru, Bolivia, and in Costa Rica and Panama in Central America.

At the close of the General Conference in Rio de Janeiro, Mrs. Holt and I went on to South Brazil, Uruguay, Argentina, Chile, Peru, and Panama. The last Sunday in July I preached in Buenos Aires. The first Sunday in August I preached in the morning at Kingston, Jamaica, and at night in Havana, Cuba. What would John Wesley think of that kind of travel? We were in Buenos Aires after the revolution in June, in which six Roman Catholic Churches in the heart of Buenos Aires were destroyed. No one could then foresee what would happen. The elimination of Juan Peron means that the Roman Catholic Church still has power. Not even Peron could crush it or separate Church and State. When I was in Argentina, I asked the President of Ward College, a Methodist College in Buenos Aires, "If you have a chance to vote this fall, will you vote for or against Peron?" His answer was, "I detest Peron and his dictatorship, but he is fighting for the separation of Church and State. For Protestants that is the most important issue in Argentina. I think I would vote for Peron." When the Roman Catholic Church has the power, it will dictate courses in religion and might even demand that priests be the teachers.

It had been ten years since I was in South America. On Victory Sunday, after the German surrender in May, 1945, I had preached at a Victory Service in our beautiful Methodist Church in downtown Buenos Aires. I stood in that same pulpit during my last trip. Ten years had brought changes in Argentina and in the rest of South America. For the most part these changes had aided rather than hurt the Methodist Church.

As an indication of its developing strength, the Brazil General Conference elected as bishops two native Brazilians, and the Methodist President of the World Council of Churches is the Methodist Bishop in Buenos Aires, with administrative authority in Bolivia, Uruguay, and Argentina.

The Methodism of Latin America is taking its place of responsibility in the Methodist family and in the larger Christian family.

II. A Visit to the Methodists of Asia

We left New York, Mrs. Holt and I, by Pan American plane on December 2, 1953. Our first stop was in London where I met with some British members of the Executive Committee of the World Methodist Council to plan meetings for the coming year, and to consult with those who should come to our Evangelistic Conference in Philadelphia June 26-28. Detained in London for four days by one of the worst fogs in the city's history, we flew to Madrid, and from there to Rome, Athens, Istanbul, Ankara, Damascus, Jerusalem, and Beirut. From Beirut we had a long flight to New Delhi, India, by way of Basra, Iraq, and Karachi, Pakistan. There in India we contacted the first Methodists we had seen since leaving London.

In New Delhi we were the guests of Bishop and Mrs. J. Waskom Pickett, and those early days in India were filled with interesting experiences. It was Christmas Eve when we reached New Delhi, and that afternoon we drove out in the country ten miles to speak at a service in one of the villages and to baptize fourteen children at a service in Christ Methodist Church at New Delhi. Then I preached at a service an hour later. Never have I faced such a congregation on Christmas Day; there were eight hundred people in the church, and twelve hundred outside in the churchyard, listening through amplifiers placed in the door and windows. Hindus and Moslems recognize Christmas as a big day, and our Christians go to church in great numbers. This was my first contact with our Indian Methodists.

The first American Methodist missionary to India went to Bareilly in 1856; and there we have not only the church but a hospital, an orphanage, schools, and a theological seminary—all offering a very broad program of service. As we met the Methodist family there, each one of them had such close ties with many we knew here at home that we felt as though they were truly members of our household. When we celebrate the centenary of Methodist missions in 1956, this city will be an important center; and I could emphasize many phases of the service there. I could call the names of our consecrated missionaries, but will not lest I overlook a person who should be mentioned.

In Lucknow the Central Committee of the World Council was entertained in Isabella Thoburn College. We Methodists were proud of the institution and happy for church leaders from all over the world and from many denominations to see the finest college for women in India. The Woman's Society of Christian Service cannot boast too much of the buildings or the instruction. The president of the college at the time was one of the presidents of the World Council of Churches, and is one of the world's great women. In Lucknow is a school for boys, and they were just completing the construction of a new chapel. In both of these schools the trustees require that at least fifty per cent of the student body shall be Christian, though Hindus and Moslems beg for admission in larger numbers than the schools can take. The meeting of the Central Committee of the World Council of Churches was recognized and honored by visits from the Governor of the Province, the Vice-President of India, and Mr. Nehru, each of whom spoke. The Methodists at the meeting of the Committee were the Principal of Wesley College in Sydney, Australia; the Reverend D. T. Niles of Ceylon; the Reverend E. C. Urwin of Great Britain; and the Reverend Frank Northam of Ireland, who is Treasurer of the World Council of Churches; in addition to the five representatives from The Methodist Church in the United States—Bishop G. Bromley Oxnam, Bishop James C. Baker, Dr. Ralph W. Sockman, Mr. C. C. Parlin, and this writer.

It was necessary to stop at both Nagpur and Hyderabad as we went to Bangalore for the South Asia Central Conference of the Methodist Church. Nagpur is the home of the daughter of Dr. John R. Mott. She is married to a Justice of the Supreme Court of India. We went to her home to inquire about Dr. Mott, who had

been seriously ill. In Nagpur we were the guests of the National
Christian Council, whose headquarters are in that city and one of
whose secretaries is a Methodist. Bishop G. Bromley Oxnam and I
had the privilege of conducting a service of Holy Communion in the
chapel at Isabella Thoburn College at the meeting of the Central
Committee of the World Council of Churches. In the years since
the organization of the World Council at Amsterdam in 1948, this
was the first and only time there has been a Methodist Service of
Holy Communion at a World Council meeting.

As I think back over the sessions of the Central Conference at
Bangalore, these impressions last:

(a) The debates and discussions were of a high order and would
    have been a credit to any Methodist Conference anywhere;
(b) The bishops and the officers of the Conference conducted its
    business in a most efficient way;
(c) The consecration and devotion of our Indian Methodists,
    preachers and laymen, were apparent in every service.

Perhaps the most important issue discussed was a plan of church
union for North India. When the South India United Church was
formed in 1947, British Methodists entered it, but American Methodists had little work in its area. The American Methodists in North
India are negotiating with Anglicans, British Baptists, and the
present United Church made up of Congregationalists and Presbyterians. The report of the Conference Committee at Bangalore recommended certain verbal changes in the Plan of Union to make it
more acceptable to Methodists but urged support. I was glad that
I was present for that able discussion. The various sections of the
report were approved by a majority of at least two-thirds to three-
fourths of those voting. The sections that caused most discussion
were the ones dealing with what we may call supplemental ordination and the one granting to the Methodist Commission authority
to speak for the Methodist Church in India without referring the
plan back to the Central Conference. In discussing supplemental
ordination all the arguments were heard one would hear in the

United States against a laying on of hands by Anglican bishops, but those Methodists in India decided that they would accept that since there were such strong reasons for union. An able layman from Calcutta influenced the decision by a striking story. This was the story:

"A Hindu had in his family a wife and son. His wife had a cat of which she was very fond and no one ever punished that cat. When the family assembled for worship in the courtyard, the Hindu came with his bowl of milk and his bowl of rice as offerings for the gods. While they were bowed in prayer, the cat would drink up the milk. He could not punish the cat, and he was puzzled. One day he got a string and tied the cat to a post before the worship and after that all went well. When the son was grown, the mother told the father that he should let the son conduct family worship. So the morning came for the son to officiate. The cat had died. The son came with his bowl of rice and his bowl of milk, but before he began the worship he suddenly jumped up and ran away. His parents thought he was embarrassed, but he soon came back with an alley cat under his arm. This cat he tied to the post and then went on with his worship. The Methodists who are so hesitant about hands laid on their heads in supplemental ordination are dragging in the cat, in my thinking, and they are just as obstinate in their opinions as the Anglicans are in their insistence on the proper episcopal succession. Do we really want union? Is it necessary in India? If we want it we will not stand back on the supplemental ordination by bishops who want to lay hands on our heads."

The decision of the Pope to name a Roman Catholic Cardinal for India and the threat of anti-Christian forces are two potent reasons for the necessity of union, in the thinking of those who favor it.

When we were at lunch with the American Consul General in Calcutta, and he knew that we were going next to Burma, he said to us, "Stay in Rangoon since the Terrorists are causing a lot of trouble in the country and along the highways." Most of our Methodist work is in the vicinity of Rangoon, but we have an important work in Pegu, a city 56 miles away. Our missionaries thought it safe to go there, and we had an undisturbed trip along the road. So we saw all of our work in Burma except a small mountain station north of Rangoon, and we met all our missionaries except those away on furlough. In addition to this, we came to know our Burmese and Chinese leaders. While in Rangoon, we had a long visit with the missionary secretaries of the British Methodist Church who had just completed a tour of Northern Burma, where their stations are located north of Mandalay. With their account of their journey I had a complete picture of our Methodism in all of Burma. The political situation is complicated still further by the presence in Northern Burma of Chinese Nationalist forces who fled across the border when the Communists took over in that part of China along the Burmese border. The presence of these Chinese Nationalists in Burma might be made an excuse by Chinese Communists to cross the border to punish and capture the Nationalists. Should Red China decide to enter Burma with force, this nation could be easily overrun. The Communists would not meet as much resistance as the Japanese did in World War II. That threat disturbs the government and is a matter of grave anxiety to our church leaders. Our Methodists in Burma are truly on the front line in the struggle of Christianity with Communism for the soul of Asia. The Terrorists who disturb the country now probably slip in from China—certainly their leaders do.

In Malaya, which is a land of tropical beauty and which reaches down almost to the Equator, the Methodist Church is the major Protestant body. From Penang in the north to Singapore on the south we saw all of our principal Methodist stations. In a conversation with the Assistant High Commissioner in the Malay Confederation I heard these words, "We may have to ask the Methodist Church and the Roman Catholic Church to take over the training of our teachers in Malayan Schools. Each church could establish a teacher-training college and the Government would help to subsidize them. These two churches are the only ones in Malay strong enough to do the job. We have been sending 250 teachers to England each year for training but that is too expensive." Two things are significant in that statement. One is the recognition of the position of the Methodist Church, and the other is the willingness of the Government to have churches conduct teacher-training courses. The Government has for years contributed generously in the erection of our Methodist schools, which are housed in very imposing school buildings. Not once has the Government sought to influence policies or interfere with teaching in our schools.

The population of Malaya is forty per cent Malay, forty per cent Chinese, and twenty per cent Indian. So we have churches for the three language groups. One Sunday afternoon I preached in one of our Chinese churches in Singapore. After my sermon in English, the Chinese pastor spoke to a church full of Chinese in Malay, summarizing the sermon for those who did not understand English. The explanation is that many of these Chinese were born in Malaya and do not know Chinese.

The struggle between Chinese and Malayan cultures constitutes a great problem, and we have separate conferences for these two groups.

The High Commissioner in Malaya has done a great job in ridding the peninsula of Communist Terrorists. For the protection of the people he has established 420 new villages and enclosed them with barbed wire. In these villages he has established schools for which he wants teachers, and is striving to build a wholesome community life. The way is open for churches to enter. Here and in all Malaya the Methodist Church has a great opportunity, and there, as in Burma, Methodists are in the front line on the border of Red China.

As we returned by the Pacific, we spent a few days in Hong Kong. Bishop and Mrs. Ralph Ward came over from Formosa to be with us, and we had many conversations about the responsibility of Methodism in that city. The Baptists and the Roman Catholics have built housing units called Friendship Villages. The Government and private individuals are building houses, but all this is inadequate to meet the need.

There were several meetings with British Methodist leaders in Hong Kong and with the visitors from the Mission House in London, whom we had met earlier in Burma, about our Methodist responsibility in the crowded city. Bishop Ward and I sent an urgent cable to the Board of Missions in New York, and American Methodism has responded by building a church and additional housing units.

CHAPTER VII

THE CHURCH OF WHICH WE DREAM

THE Methodist Church of the United States is conscious of the divisions in Christendom, as is the Methodist Church in every land. Even in the Methodist family in America there are still divisions. In the World Methodist Council are the Free Methodist Church, the Primitive Methodist Church, and the Wesleyan Methodist Church—all smaller Methodist Churches in the American Methodist family. Then there are three very large Methodist Churches among the Negroes in America, which are independent of one another and independent of the Methodist Church. How soon it will be before negotiations for union can be begun between the Methodist Church and the three smaller or the three larger Methodist churches, no one can prophesy. In the years since the Oxford Conference of World Methodism, I have brought together several times representative bishops of the African Methodist Episcopal Church, the African Methodist Episcopal Zion Church, and the Christian Methodist Church. These Negro leaders are aware of the pressure of the Roman Catholic Church on the one side and the fanatical sects on the other. They realize that in this situation there ought to be increasing understanding among these independent Negro Methodist Churches, and that they should begin to think about negotiations for union that will enable them to present a united front. Perhaps the Methodist Church of the World may overtake our slow progress in American Methodism and bring all Methodist churches at the same time, whether large or small, into one great church. Should that be the church of which we dream?

Turning to a discussion of the Greenwich Plan for larger Protestant Union in the United States, there are some facts about the history of that Plan and its proposals that should be of interest to

Methodists everywhere. The initial inspiration for this plan of church union came at the biennial meeting of the Congregational Christian General Council held at Grinnell, Iowa, in June, 1946. A resolution was unanimously adopted at that meeting requesting the Federal Council of Churches to invite those denominations which "recognize one another's ministries and sacraments" to send officially appointed representatives to a plenary conference to explore the possibility of a closer union. This proposal was seconded in the following August by the International Convention of the Disciples of Christ, which somewhat broadened the invitation to include "those communions which are in sufficient accord in essentials of Christian faith and order to give promise that such a conference would result in further and effectual achievement of Christian unity."

Whereupon, the invitation was formally transmitted to each of the 24 constituent denominations of the Federal Council, and others not affiliated with it. Nine denominations responded favorably as follows: Methodist, Presbyterian U.S.A., Presbyterian U.S., Congregational Christian, Disciples of Christ, Evangelical and Reformed, African Methodist Episcopal, Colored Methodist Episcopal, and the Association of Community Churches. These bodies represent about 16 million members, or nearly 40% of American Protestantism.

Their appointed representatives met at Greenwich, Connecticut, in December, 1949. During three days of deliberation, it was unanimously decided that they should seek for nothing less than "an organic union" of their several bodies, "a fellowship and organization of the church which will enable it to act as one body under Jesus Christ who is the Head of the Church." The conference organized itself as a continuing body, to be called, simply, "The Conference on Church Union." Bishop Ivan Lee Holt of the Methodist Church was elected president; the Reverend Dr. William B. Pugh, stated clerk of the General Assembly of the Presbyterian Church U.S.A., vice-president; the Reverend Dr. John Lentz, Evangelical and Reformed Church, treasurer. The Reverend Dr. Douglas Horton, minister of the Congregational Christian General Council, accepted the task of acting secretary. A Drafting Committee was appointed to draw up a Plan of Union. Two members from each participating denomination were named to constitute such a committee, together with members of the Executive Committee, ex officio.

The first meeting of the Drafting Committee was held at Randolph, New Hampshire, in July, 1950. During four days of intensive deliberations, a Plan of Union was drawn up which received the approval of the entire committee. The Reverend Dr. Pugh contributed largely to the drafting of the Plan. His tragic death two months later removed from the undertaking one of its wisest and most ardent advocates. A second meeting of the Drafting Committee reviewed the Plan and presented it to a plenary session of the Conference on Church Union in New York, in October, 1950, where, with minor changes, it was approved for advisory submission to a joint convocation of the Conference on Church Union and several commissions on inter-church relations of the nine denominations.

This convocation, consisting of 75 representatives of the nine denominations, was held in Cincinnati, Ohio, in January, 1951. The Plan was thoroughly discussed. No formal action was taken or requested, though the sentiment was strongly favorable and helpful. Three denominational groups—Methodist, Congregational, and Disciples of Christ—met separately and presented to the convocation memoranda containing assurances of hearty approval of the Plan, together with certain suggestions for its improvement. The Reverend Dr. Gaines M. Cook, Executive Secretary of the International Convention of Disciples of Christ, was elected secretary of the Conference on Church Union.

A meeting of the Drafting Committee was held in New York in March, 1951, at which all the suggestions for amendment proposed at Cincinnati were earnestly considered. Some of these were incorporated in the Plan, others were included with modifications, still others were felt to be either unnecessary or inconsistent with the Plan. A further meeting of the Drafting Committee was held in New York in November, 1952. After intensive consideration of the text of the Plan of Union resulting in numerous minor revisions, it was deemed ready to submit to a plenary session of the Conference on Church Union. This session was held at Greenwich in May, 1953. Two days were devoted to a critical examination and interpretation of the Plan and discussion of methods for securing similar consideration from a widely representative cross section of the churches. For this purpose the Plan is now submitted to the commissions on Christian Unity of the several churches and other church organizations and groups, including theological seminaries, for study and recommendation.

The plan of Union worked out by the Conference on Church Union embodies the polities of the Congregational, the Episcopal, and the Presbyterian forms of church organization. The detailed plan I do not give, but I want to quote some words that indicate our spirit and convictions.

In considering the Plan of Union it is important that it be taken, not as a final, comprehensive, or adequate plan, but as a kind of line drawing of a possible united church. The fundamental problem which it seeks to solve is that of bringing into one body three types of churches which already recognize one another's ministries and sacraments but are accustomed to operate under somewhat different forms of organization. These forms are usually designated as congregational, espiscopal, and presbyterian. Previous plans for union have largely attempted to merge these polities by compromising or eliminating their differences. The distinctive characteristic of the present plan is that the essential features of these polities are preserved and maintained simultaneously within the one church.

In our many conferences together we have reached the heartening conclusion that in their actual functioning, quite aside from traditional theory, these three types of organization are more similar than is commonly assumed. The congregational group of churches is more like the non-congregational, the episcopal more like the non-episcopal, and the presbyterian more like the non-presbyterian groups than any of them has supposed the others to be. The recognition of this fact has made it possible to bring the three types of organization together in a Plan of Union which provides for the continuance of all three.

The Plan is offered to the churches, not with the expectation that they will at once commit themselves to union under it, but in the hope that they may be able to adopt it "in principle" with whatever recommendations they may suggest for its improvement and completion. It is conceived as a minimum structure upon which, if its essential principles are favorably received, further action may be undertaken to consummate the union here envisaged.

Questions will, no doubt, arise concerning matters of procedure within the framework of this Plan. Many such questions have arisen in our deliberations, but they have been put aside in the interest of presenting as simply as possible an over-all picture of what a united church might be. We ask that the Plan be given careful study and that both official and informal groups will crystallize their opinions as to (1) the desirability and (2) the practicability of union on the principles embodied in the Plan. Such expressions of opinion will guide the Conference on Church Union in its further deliberations.

In the preamble to the Plan the representatives of the churches say:

"We, the Conference on Church Union, consisting of officially appointed representatives of our several churches, gratefully recognize the initiative and guidance of God in the movement among Christian people for a united Church. The call for unity is a divine imperative and we believe that union is an indispensable means to that end.

"We have long known that in essentials of faith we are already one. We now rejoice in the growing realization that the practical operations of our several polities are strikingly similar. Over many years there has been a steady growth of fraternal fellowship, mutual co-operation, and the spirit of unity among us. This has prompted us earnestly and prayerfully to inquire what may be the next step in the development of our responsibility for one another. Through our common faith in Jesus Christ as Lord and Saviour we are made one body in Him and, in penitence for our present unhappy separation from one another, we believe that our Master now calls us to transcend those barriers which divide us into various and often competing denominations and churches."

The statement of the common faith to which the Greenwich Conference came in its plan is this:

WE ARE ONE in common faith of the Christian Church and in our desire to share as a common heritage the various historic and treasured expressions of that faith.

WE ARE ONE in our common belief

in God our Father;

in Jesus Christ, his only Son, our Savior;

in the Holy Spirit, our Guide and Comforter;

in the Holy Catholic Church, through which God's eternal purpose of salvation is proclaimed and His Kingdom comes on earth;

in the Scriptures of the Old and New Testaments as disclosing the Word of God for men, from which new light is evermore breaking forth for us and for our world;

in the forgiveness of sins;

and in the life everlasting.

WE ARE ONE in our faith that the Church is of God and in the deepening sense of obligation with which we hear the prayer of our Lord for his disciples, "That they all may be one; even as thou, Father, art in me, and I in thee, that they also may be one in us: that the world may believe that thou hast sent me."

WE ARE ONE in that spirit of love which, owning the same Lord, recognizes diversity of gifts, concerns, and ministrations, and assures to all freedom in ways of worship, and of witness.

WE ARE ONE in our purpose that this United Church of Christ be dedicated to our Lord for the furtherance of His redemptive work in the world.

In the discussion of Union between The Methodist Church of the United States and the Protestant Episcopal Church, the Commission on Approaches to Union made a proposal to the Methodist Commission on Union. That proposal, as it was outlined to the General Convention of the Protestant Episcopal Church, is this:

"The Commission cannot conceive of a real intercommunion without an arrangement of inter-celebration, and the sharing of the historic episcopate seems to be a necessary prerequisite for the authorization of inter-celebration. The Commission, however, is concerned lest this be understood to suggest a mechanical concept of the ministry rather than an appreciation of the historic ministry in the ongoing life of the Church. While the arrangement worked out in the Philippines with the Aglipayan Church has stimulated our thinking in this area, we feel it necessary to point out that any sharing of the historic episcopate involves mutually accepted 'undertakings and commitments,' if it is really to be a step toward intercommunion and eventually reunion.

"The Commission's thinking along this line is in the direction of what might be necessary in achieving intercommunion with the Methodist Church. We are exploring the possibility of an arrangement based on first reaching mutually accepted 'undertakings and commitments' by which when new Methodist bishops are consecrated following one of the Quadrennial General Conferences of that body, three Anglican bishops or three bishops of some other Communion with historic succession take part in the consecration. Certainly such a suggestion raises other questions which must be answered. What about a reciprocal arrangement for the consecration of the Episcopal bishops? What about the already ordained clergy in both Churches? The process is a little simpler to envision where the Methodist Church is concerned because all new bishops of that body, as we understand it, are consecrated following its General Conference and not individually from time to time and at different places, as is usually the case with us.

"It is our thought that such an arrangement would be a crucial step in making it possible for the Episcopal Church and the Methodist Church to live side by side in intercommunion, yet as separate bodies, until such time as the two Churches have sufficiently interpenetrated each other as to make reunion spiritually and administratively meaningful.

"The Commission realizes that, before any such arrangement is completed, there should be a consultation with the Lambeth Conference as well as legislative action by the General Convention.

"At a joint meeting on April 28, 1955, the Commission presented a proposal to the Commission on Union of the Methodist Church, suggesting a way by which intercommunion might be effected and some of the steps necessary to bring it about. The proposal was for discussion only and does not represent the final thinking of the Episcopal Commission. It had to do primarily with bringing the Methodist bishops within the historic episcopate. The Episcopal Commission invited the Methodist negotiators to prepare a counter suggestion to be considered at the next joint meeting of the two commissions. The joint meeting also considered the Faith and Order statement, as prepared by this Commission and received by Lambeth in 1948 and the General Convention of 1949.

"Following the joint meeting of the Commissions, an informal session was held, involving eleven bishops of the Protestant Episcopal Church and eight bishops of the Methodist Church, in order that there might be mutual discussion and consultation, both as regards the proposal and the Faith and Order statement. The bishops' meeting covered much of the same material as the joint meeting of the two Commissions. There was a strong consensus that the project was valuable and should be repeated."

The Methodist answer to this proposal is this:

"And now concerning the Proposal: The Methodist and Protestant Episcopal Churches have so much in common that it hardly behooves either one to find much fault with the other. We have a common history. We have both stemmed from the Church of England. Until 172 years ago, we were both a component part of the Church of England. The separation from the Mother Church, and the setting up of our respective ecclesiastical organizations in America were the effects of a common cause, viz: the success of the American revolution. We both acknowledge the Scriptures as the rule and standard of faith and life. We accept the same Articles of Religion, repeat the same creeds, sing the same hymns, use practically the same ritual in marriage and burial, in baptism and the Lord's Supper. We have the same form of church government. We both have bishops and use the same ritual in consecrating them. We are so nearly alike and have so much in common that it seems strange that one would have to reckon that it will take 30 to 40 years to remove the barriers that separate us. It would seem that if a clear-headed and straight-thinking delegate to the General Conference of the Methodist Church—a delegate in whose devoted religion and common sense his fellow churchmen had confidence—and a like-minded and similarly endowed delegate to the Protestant Episcopal General Convention should arise in their respective gatherings, and should state the valid reasons for union, and declare that the only way to unite is to unite, and then move that the two churches be united in the shortest time possible consistent with the constitutional procedures of the respective churches, and let the differences dissolve in the fervent prayer, the radiant fellowship, the spiritual glow, and the passionate devotion to our Divine Lord and His cause which would result from the prayerful, disinterested, unselfish spirit which would animate the movement, the motion would be adopted and the union would be consummated!

"But it is not likely that such a motion will be made, or that the leadership of the respective churches would consent to such quick work, even in order to expunge the scandal of disunion! Therefore, let us look at some of the hurdles to be overcome.

"We come now to the consideration of the 'plan looking to organic unity' of the Methodist and the Protestant Episcopal Churches, as submitted by our Episcopal brethren.

"1st. 'At all subsequent consecrations of Methodist Bishops three or more Bishops of churches in the historic Episcopal succession participate in the laying on of hands.'

"2nd. 'It would be agreed that at a specified time all future ordinations of 'elders' in the Methodist Church would be at the hands of Methodist bishops consecrated in the historic succession.'

"3rd. 'The time required for the achievement of a completely episcopally ordained ministry would be longer than the anticipated 30 or 40 years.'

"4th. 'The form of Ordination to be followed by Methodist bishops in the future would ... substitute the word *priest* or *presbyter* for *elder*.'

" (The foregoing four 'points' are the gist of the plan; but the 'Proposal for Discussion,' from which they are extracted, should be read carefully in its entirety.)

"What have the Methodists to say in response to these four points?

"1st. Let us admit that each Church has something to contribute which will make the united church greater than either the Methodist or Protestant Episcopal Church is alone. The Episcopal Church has its connection with Anglicanism, and through it with the Historic Episcopate; an emphasis upon worship, with artistic concomitants; a following in the American population which is sensitive both to ceremonialism and also to 'prestige.'

"The Methodist Church has its record of evangelistic achievement; its numerical strength, being the largest Protestant Church in America; its leadership in social reform; its contribution to civic life—so great that Lord Bryce declared that no man could know America until he knew the Methodist Church, and that it, more nearly than any other, is the 'National church'; its emphasis upon education, having founded more colleges and universities that are still in existence than any other Denomination; its stress upon the virtue of abstemiousness; its millions of dollars for world service; and its insistence that Christian religion is more truly indicated by life and experience than by mere intellectual assent to creedal dogma and fidelity to form.

"God has greatly honored the Protestant Episcopal Church and has put the stamp of His approval upon its Ministry. In no less degree, God has honored the Methodist Church, and has placed His imprimatur upon its Ministry.

"Therefore, let us move as rapidly as possible toward complete union, and in our preliminary forms let us so conduct ourselves that neither Church shall appear to be regarded as either superior or inferior to the other. To that end, let a plan of unification be prepared which will offer the following solution of the vexatious problem which we have been considering here, to wit:

"1st. Let it be agreed that at the appropriate time, and as a condition to union, all the bishops of the two churches will carefully arrange for and hold a meeting which will be characterized by dignity and deep reverence, and which will be a witness to the world that the Episcopal leadership recognizes that a new dedication of themselves, a new consecration, is appropriate to the harmonious and successful direction of the newly united churches' administrative affairs.

"2nd. Then let the ceremony of that new dedication be a consecration of the Methodist Bishops by the Protestant Episcopal Bishops, and of the Protestant Episcopal Bishops by the Methodist Bishops—the words of consecration in each case being accompanied by the laying on of hands.

"3rd. Then let the Bishops hold consecration services in their respective dioceses or areas, in which services the ministers (priests or elders) shall be invited, though not required, to receive the laying on of the hands of the Bishops.

"Let this be considered as a program that will accomplish all that is aimed at in the 'Proposal for Discussion' in considerably less than 30 or 40 years, and doubtless with considerably less irritation, and without creating 'inferiority complexes' which would assert themselves as increased barriers between these two churches which are so much alike and which God has so signally owned and honored."

So do we Methodists move toward one Holy Catholic Church.

PART II

The World Methodist Council

by

Elmer T. Clark

CHAPTER VIII

DEVELOPMENT OF THE WORLD METHODIST COUNCIL

On MAY 31, 1876, the General Conference of the Methodist Episcopal Church in the United States, meeting at Baltimore, adopted a resolution proposing an "Oecumenical Conference of Methodism" and asked the bishops to name a committee of nine persons to consider the matter and contact the Methodist bodies of every land with reference thereto. The secretary of that committee, the Rev. Dr. A. C. George, corresponded with the various groups in the United States; and at a meeting at Philadelphia in May, 1878, the committee addressed a communication to the British Wesleyan Conference at Bradford, which was transmitted by the fraternal delegate, Chancellor E. O. Haven.

The original action of the General Conference had suggested that the proposed Ecumenical gathering should be composed of the Methodist organizations that "accept the Arminian theology, and maintain usages which distinguish them to some extent from every other denomination of Christians." The committee enumerated twenty-four groups in the United States, Canada, Great Britain, France, and Australia which might be included. It also suggested that the Conference should consider such topics as the following: Methodist doctrines, the ministry and other means of evangelization, home missions and Sunday schools, education in Church and State, intemperance and social evils, publications, foreign missions, perils from the papacy and infidelity, and the resources of Methodism for the work of Christ.

The communication was favorably received, and the British Conference of 1878 named a committee to consider the proposal and report the following year. This committee entered into correspondence with the American group and recommended to the British Conference at Birmingham in August, 1879, the calling of an Ecumenical Methodist Conference. It was proposed that the gathering should be held in London in 1882 and that the membership should be limited to 650, the Wesleyan Methodists and American Methodists each having 250 representatives. It was further proposed that foreign delegates should be given hospitality but should bear their own travelling expenses.

In its official reply to the American proposal, the British Conference pointed out some difficulties in the plan as submitted. It stated,

"The plan assumes that there is such a substantial community among various bodies descended from the English Methodism of John Wesley, that all may be regarded as virtually 'one people,' distinguished into sections, which only vary from each other in matters quite subordinate and almost insignificant. We are bound to say that to us there appears to be a certain unreality about this view. . . . No such virtual identity is found among the different ecclesiastical bodies enumerated in your communication. They do not acknowledge the same standard of doctrine, and characteristic differences are found in their exposition even of doctrines which are nominally held in common."

Mention was made of divergences in relation to class meetings, church membership, and church government. "Mere Arminianism in theology does not suffice,—nor even evangelical and experimental Arminianism—to define a Methodist Church." Therefore, continued the British statement, these differences should be frankly recognized and excluded from the discussions.

The General Conference of the Methodist Episcopal Church, South, meeting in Atlanta in May, 1878, approved the proposed Ecumenical Conference and instructed the bishops to appoint a committee of seven persons to represent the Church in arranging for the Conference and to appoint the delegates thereto.

A joint committee of American Methodists was set up, and at a meeting in Cincinnati on May 10, 1880, this committee issued a call for the Conference. The call stated that the assembly would not be for legislative purposes, and it repeated the topics which it regarded as proper for consideration. It further stated that the Conference should be composed of 400 members, of which 200 were assigned to British and Continental Methodism and their mission fields, and a similar number to the Churches in the United States and Canada. It further stated that the representation should be composed of an equal number of clerical and lay delegates. A general executive committee was recommended. This was to consist of a minister and a layman from each Methodist body and would be divided into Eastern and Western Sections. On November 4, 1880, a meeting of the Methodists of Great Britain and Ireland met in London and unanimously concurred in the plan.

The First Ecumenical Methodist Conference—1881

The First Ecumenical Methodist Conference assembled on Wednesday, September 7, 1881, in the City Road Chapel at London. The delegates represented 28 different denominations from 20 different sections of the world. There were numerous Negro delegates from several Negro Methodist churches, but the Volume of Proceedings issued by the Conference pointed out that there was in attendance "no African born and residing in Africa, nor any native Asiatic, American Indian, or Polynesian."

The churches and the number of representatives appointed to this First Ecumenical Conference were as follows:

Eastern Section

Wesleyan Methodist Church 86
Irish Methodist Church 10
Methodist New Connexion 12
Primitive Methodist Church 36
Bible Christian Church 10
United Methodist Free Church 22
Wesleyan Reform Union 4

United Free Gospel Church 2
French Methodist Church 2
Australian Methodist Church 16

Western Section

Methodist Episcopal Church 78
Methodist Episcopal Church, South 36
Methodist Protestant Church 6
Evangelical Association 2
United Brethren 2
American Wesleyan Church 2
Free Methodist Church 2
Primitive Methodist Church in the U.S. 2
Independent Methodist Church 2
Congregational Methodist Church 2
African Methodist Episcopal Church 12
African Methodist Episcopal Zion Church 10
Colored Methodist Episcopal Church 6
Methodist Church of Canada 12
Methodist Episcopal Church of Canada 4
Primitive Methodist Church of Canada 2
Canadian Bible Christian 2
British Methodist Episcopal Church of Canada 2

The record indicates that nearly all of these delegates actually attended, although there were no representatives from the American Wesleyan Church, the Free Methodist Church, and the Congregational Methodist Church, and only one attended from the Colored Methodist Episcopal Church. Of the total number actually designated, however, only thirty failed to attend. Of course, the actual attendance, including the visitors, was very large.

On the opening day the most conspicuous laymen, Sir William McArthur, Lord Mayor of London, received the delegates at the Mansion House. Three large central meetings were held at Exeter

Hall, and numerous meetings were held in the various Methodist Chapels of London. The opening service was conducted by the Rev. R. George Osborn, President of the British Wesleyan Conference, and the sermon was preached by Bishop Matthew Simpson, the senior Bishop of the Methodist Episcopal Church, U. S. A.

This First Ecumenical Methodist Conference had no executive functions and was devoted entirely to public addresses and fellowship. This indeed was true of the first seven such gatherings. The Conference set up four divisions, namely, the British Wesleyan Methodist Church, the other British Churches, the Episcopal Methodist Churches in the United States and Canada, and the non-Episcopal Churches in the United States and Canada. The presiding officers were selected day by day, being drawn alternately from these divisions. A business committee was organized to direct the Conference, and papers presented in the regular sessions were limited to twenty minutes in length.

A Secretary from each of the divisions was appointed as follows: The Rev. John Bond of the Wesleyan Methodist Church; the Rev. J. S. Withington of the United Free Church; the Rev. A. C. George, D.D., of the Methodist Episcopal Church; and the Rev. S. B. Southerland, D.D., of the Methodist Protestant Church.

The presiding officers were the Rev. George Osborn, D.D., of the British Wesleyan Church; Bishop Jesse T. Peck of the Methodist Episcopal Church; the Rev. J. Stacey, D.D., of the Methodist New Connexion; the Rev. S. B. Southerland, D.D., of the Methodist Protestant Church; the Rev. E. E. Jenkins of the Wesleyan Methodist Church; Bishop H. N. McTyeire, D.D., of the Methodist Episcopal Church, South; the Rev. Charles Kendall of the Primitive Methodist Church; the Rev. George Douglas, LL.D., of the Methodist Church of Canada; the Rev. William Arthur, M.A., of the Wesleyan Methodist Church; Bishop Daniel A. Payne, D.D., of the African Methodist Episcopal Church; the Rev. R. Chew, of the United Methodist Free Churches; the Rev. Henry Pope, D.D., of the Methodist Church of Canada.

93

The outstanding subjects for discussion and the principal speakers were as follows:

Second day, September 8: *Methodism: Its History and Results*: The Rev. William Cooke, D.D., Methodist New Connexion of Great Britain; the Rev. W. X. Ninde, D.D., Methodist Episcopal Church; the Rev. Arthur Edwards, D.D., Methodist Episcopal Church; the Rev. M. C. Osborn, Secretary to the British Wesleyan Missionary Society; the Rev. W. Arthur, M.A., British Wesleyan Methodist Church; the Rev. Bishop L. H. Holsey, Colored Methodist Episcopal Church of America; the Rev. Alpheus W. Wilson, D.D., Methodist Episcopal Church, South; and the Rev. S.S. Barton, United Methodist Free Churches of Great Britain.

Third Day, September 9: *Evangelical Agencies of Methodism*: The Rev. S. Antliff, D.D., Primitive Methodist Church of Great Britain, the Rev. J. B. McFerrin, D.D., Methodist Episcopal Church, South; Hon. J. W. F. White, Methodist Episcopal Church; Mr. W. Shepherd Allen, M.P., British Wesleyan Methodist Church; the Rev. F. W. Bourne, Bible Christian Churches of Great Britain; the Rev. Charles H. Payne, D.D., Methodist Episcopal Church; the Rev. John P. Newman, D.D., LL.D., Methodist Episcopal Church; and the Rev. J. Stacey, D.D., President, Methodist New Connexion of Great Britain.

Fourth Day, September 10: *Methodism and the Young*: The Rev. Joseph Wood, M.A., Primitive Methodist Church of Great Britain; the Rev. J. Mc. H. Farley, Methodist Episcopal Zion Church; the Rev. H. A. Thompson, D.D., United Brethren Church; and Mr. G. J. Smith, British Wesleyan Methodist Church.

Fifth Day, September 12: *Methodism and the Lord's Day*: The Rev. John Baker, M.A., British Wesleyan Methodist Church; the Rev. B. T. Roberts, Free Methodist Church of America; the Rev. Bishop D. A. Payne, African Methodist Episcopal Church; the Rev. Joseph Kirsop, United Methodist Free Churches of Great Britain; the Rev. Charles Garrett, British Wesleyan Methodist Church; the Rev. Marshall W. Taylor, Methodist Episcopal Church; the Rev.

J. M. Walden, D.D., LL.D., Methodist Episcopal Church; and Mr. William Beckworth, Primitive Methodist Church of Great Britain.

Sixth Day, September 13: *Possible Perils of Methodism:* The Rev. J. Guttridge, United Methodist Free Churches of Great Britain; the Rev. E. B. Ryckman, D.D., Methodist Church of Canada; the Rev. Daniel Curry, D.D., Methodist Episcopal Church; the Rev. W. L. Watkinson, British Wesleyan Methodist Church; the Rev. J. W. McKay, D.D., Irish Methodist Church, the Rev. Charles M. Giffin, Independent Methodist Church; the Rev. Bishop J. P. Thompson, Methodist Episcopal Zion Church; and the Rev. R. Cheesman, Primitive Methodist Church of Great Britain.

Seventh Day, September 14: *Education:* Mr. T. G. Osborn, M.A., British Wesleyan Methodist Church; the Rev. F. A. Mood, D.D., Methodist Episcopal Church, South; the Rev. C. G. Andrews, D.D., Methodist Episcopal Church, South; the Rev. G. W. Olver, B.A., British Wesleyan Methodist Church; the Rev. W. B. Pope, D.D., British Wesleyan Methodist Church; the Rev. George R. Crooks, D.D., Methodist Episcopal Church; the Rev. E. J. Badgeley, D.D., LL.D., Methodist Episcopal Church of Canada; and the Rev. J. Dymond, Bible Christian Church of Great Britain.

Eight Day, September 15: *The Use of the Press for the Advancement of Christianity:* The Rev. J. Swann Withington, United Free Methodist Churches of Great Britain; the Rev. J. Cooper Antliff, M.A., B.D., Primitive Methodist Church of Canada; the Rev. C. K. Marshall, D.D., Methodist Episcopal Church, South; the Rev. H. W. Holland, British Wesleyan Methodist Church; the Rev. George Osborn, D.D., British Wesleyan Methodist Church; and the Rev. James A. Buckley, D.D., Methodist Episcopal Church.

Ninth Day, September 16: *Home Missions:* Mr. John Macdonald, Methodist Church of Canada; the Rev. Hugh Gilmore, Primitive Methodist Church of Great Britain; Mr. T. H. Bainbridge, British Wesleyan Methodist Church; the Rev. G. B. McElroy, D.D., Methodist Protestant Church; the Rev. S. B. Southerland, D.D., Methodist Protestant Church; the Rev. Richard Green, British Wesleyan

Methodist Church; the Rev. T. B. Stephenson, B.A., LL.D., British Wesleyan Methodist Church; and the Rev. Jacob Todd, D.D., Methodist Episcopal Church.

Tenth Day, September 17: *Foreign Missions:* The Rev. John M. Reid, D.D., Methodist Episcopal Church; the Rev. E. E. Jenkins, M.A., British Wesleyan Methodist Church; the Rev. J. H. Rigg, D.D., British Wesleyan Methodist Church; and the Rev. R. S. Maclay, D.D., Methodist Episcopal Church.

Eleventh Day, September 19: *Foreign Missions:* The Rev. Wyman H. Potter, D.D., Methodist Episcopal Church, South; the Rev. John Kilner, British Wesleyan Methodist Church; the Rev. J. S. Banks, British Wesleyan Methodist Church; the Rev. Leroy M. Vernon, D.D., Methodist Episcopal Church; the Rev. A. Sulzberger, Ph.D., Methodist Episcopal Church; the Rev. H. J. Piggott, B.A., British Wesleyan Methodist Church; the Rev. C. C. McKechnie, Primitive Methodist Church of Great Britain; and the Rev. C. W. Miller, Methodist Episcopal Church, South.

Twelfth Day, September 20: *Christian Unity:* The Rev. Augustus C. George, D.D., Methodist Episcopal Church; the Rev. William Cocker, D.D., Methodist New Connexion Church of Great Britain; the Rev. John Myers, United Methodist Free Churches of Great Britain; Professor J. P. Shorter, African Methodist Episcopal Church; Mr. David Allison, LL.D., Methodist Church of Canada, and the Rev. Benjamin Gregory, British Wesleyan Methodist Church.

Second Ecumenical Methodist Conference—1891

The first Ecumenical Methodist Conference did not make plans for a second meeting, but in 1886 the British Conference named a committee to consider the advisability of another assemblage in 1891. The following year the Conference approved the United States as the site and transmitted the proposal to the Methodist Episcopal Church by its fraternal delegate, the Rev. C. H. Kelly. The General Conference of 1888 concurred, as did the British Conferences of 1889 and 1890. The union of Methodism in Canada had been consummated in 1883.

The Western Section decided that the Conference should be in the Metropolitan Methodist Episcopal Church in Washington. A reception was held for the delegates from the Eastern Section in the Music Hall at New York on the evening of October 4, 1891, at which addresses were made by Dr. J. M. King and Bishop C. D. Foss, with Mr. J. D. Slayback presiding. At Washington a reception was given by Honorable M. G. Emery, the ex-mayor, on the evening of October 8. On the following evening there was a reception at the Metropolitan African Episcopal Church, and on October 15, a similar event was tendered by the Trustees of the American University. There were excursions to Mount Vernon and the grounds of the American University, and a final reception at the Academy of Music in Philadelphia, at which the Postmaster of the City presided and the Mayor made an address of welcome. The high point of the social events, however, was a reception at the White House given on the afternoon of Monday, October 12, by President Benjamin Harrison and Mrs. Harrison. President Harrison also visited the Conference and delivered an address on October 17.

The Methodist bodies represented and the number of delegates were as follows:

Western Section

Methodist Episcopal Church	126
Methodist Episcopal Church, South	64
Methodist Church of Canada	24
African Methodist Episcopal Church	19
African Methodist Episcopal Zion Church	15
Colored Methodist Episcopal Church	9
Methodist Protestant Church	9
United Brethren in Christ	7
Union American Methodist Episcopal Church	3
African Union Methodist Protestant Church	3

Free Methodist Church 3
Congregational Methodist Church 3
Primitive Methodist Church 3
British Methodist Episcopal Church 3
Independent Methodist Church 2
United Brethren in Christ (Old Constitution) 2
American Wesleyan Church 6

Eastern Section

Wesleyan Methodist Church 77
Irish Methodist Church 12
Methodist New Connexion 12
Primitive Methodist Church 31
Bible Christian Church 10
United Methodist Free Church 21
French Methodist Church 2
Australasian Methodist Church 10
Independent Methodist Church 2
Wesleyan Reform Union 4
South African Methodist Church 1
West Indian Methodist Church 2

The arrangements for this Conference were similar to those of the 1881 session. There were no permanent officers. The presiding officers, of whom there were twenty-five, were chosen each day, and the four secretaries were drawn from the four divisions as in the former instance. There was no general theme, but there was a daily topic on which from six to eight addresses were delivered. These topics were: Ecumenical Methodism, The Unity and Catholicity of the Church, The Church and Scientific Thought, Church Agencies, Education, Romanism, Temperance, Social Problems, Missions, War and Peace, The Church and Public Morality, and The Outlook.

As has been true of all the Methodist World Conferences, the leaders of the Church throughout the world were selected as representatives. At the second session some notable figures who had been prominent in 1881 had now passed away, including the Rev. George Osborn, Bishop Matthew Simpson, Sir William McArthur, Bishop Jesse T. Peck, Dr. John B. McFerrin, General Clinton B. Fisk, and Washington C. DePauw.

Third Ecumenical Methodist Conference—1901

The Third Ecumenical Methodist Conference met in Wesley's Chapel on City Road in London on September 4, 1901, and continued until September 17. The Rev. William Arthur, who had edited the *Proceedings* of the two previous Conferences, had passed away at the age of eighty-two, and his task fell upon the Rev. T. Bowman Stephenson, D.D., LL.D., of the Wesleyan Methodist Church.

The rules and regulations for this Conference did not differ greatly from those of the previous Conferences. They provided that there should be 500 members, of which 300 were assigned to the Western Section and 200 to the Eastern Section. The principle of four divisions with a secretary from each was continued. The allocation of membership was as follows:

Eastern Section

Wesleyan Methodist Church	86
Irish Methodist Church	10
Methodist New Connexion	10
Primitive Methodist Church	34
Bible Christian Church	10
United Methodist Free Churches	20
French Methodist Church	2
Australasian Methodist Church	12
Independent Methodist Church	3
Wesleyan Reform Union	3
South African Methodist Church	6
West Indian Methodist Church	4

Western Section

Methodist Episcopal Church 120
Methodist Episcopal Church, South 70
Methodist Church of Canada 24
African Methodist Episcopal Church 18
African Methodist Episcopal Zion Church 14
Colored Methodist Episcopal Church 9
Methodist Protestant Church 9
African Union Methodist Protestant Church 1
Union American Methodist Episcopal Church 3
United Evangelical Church 1
Primitive Methodist Church 1
Free Methodist Church 1

The Secretaries were the Rev. John Bond, Wesleyan Methodist Church; Mr. Thomas Snape, J. P., United Methodist Free Churches; the Rev. James M. King, D.D., Methodist Episcopal Church; and Professor W. I. Shaw, D.D., LL.D., Methodist Church of Canada.

As formerly, the presiding officers were chosen day by day by the business committee. Those who presided at the various sessions were as follows: The Rev. W. T. Davison, M.A., D.D., Wesleyan Methodist Church; Bishop A. W. Wilson, D.D., Methodist Episcopal Church, South; the Rev. H. B. Kendall, B.A., Primitive Methodist Church; Bishop B. W. Arnett, D.D., African Methodist Episcopal Church; the Rev. E. J. Watkins, D.D., Australasian Methodist Church; Bishop J. H. Vincent, D.D., LL.D., Methodist Episcopal Church; the Rev. G. T. Candlin, Methodist New Connexion; the Rev. J. Luke, Bible Christian Church; Chancellor N. Burwash, D.D., Methodist Church of Canada; the Rev. D. Brook, M.A., D.C.L., United Methodist Free Churches; Bishop J. C. Hartzell, D.D., LL.D., Methodist Episcopal Church; the Rev. F. T. Tagg, D.D., Methodist Protestant Church; and the Rev. T. B. Stephenson, D.D., LL.D., Wesleyan Methodist Church.

As in the previous instances, the various churches had appointed some of their outstanding leaders as delegates. Among those whose names are more or less well-known to Methodists everywhere should be mentioned the Rev. Dr. W. T. Davison, President of the Conference; the Rev. Dr. J. Agar Beet; the Rev. Nehemiah Curnock; the Rev. Dr. J. Scott Lidgett; the Rev. Dr. James H. Riggs; the Rev. Dinsdale T. Young and Mr. Joseph Rank of the Wesleyan Methodist Church. Among those who represented the Methodist Episcopal Church were Bishops Hurst, Vincent, Hamilton, and Hartzell; the Rev. Dr. William Burt, the Rev. Dr. J. W. Butler, the Rev. Dr. Richard J. Cooke, the Rev. Dr. John A. Goucher, the Rev. Dr. W. I. Haven; Professor J. L. Nuelson and Professor C. T. Winchester.

From the Methodist Episcopal Church, South, went Bishops Galloway, Granbery, and Wilson; the Rev. Dr. Gross Alexander, the Rev. Dr. Young J. Allen, the Rev. Dr. James Atkins, the Rev. J. D. Hammond, the Rev. Dr. Elijah Embree Hoss, the Rev. Dr. J. C. Kilgo, the Rev. Dr. A. J. Lamar, the Rev. Dr. W. B. Murrah, the Rev. Dr. George C. Rankin, the Rev. Dr. A. Coke Smith, the Rev. Dr. John J. Tigert, the Rev. Dr. W. F. Tillett, Professor R. S. Hyer, and Chancellor J. H. Kirkland. In this listing will be recognized the names of persons who later became bishops and occupied other positions of prominence in their churches.

There was no general theme for this Conference. There were topics for the afternoon and morning sessions, and many of these were subdivided into subjects on which addresses were made. The main topics which occupied attention were as follows: Ecumenical Methodism; the Influence of Methodism in the Promotion of International Peace; Methodism and Christian Unity; Modern Biblical Criticism; Protestantism versus Modern Sacerdotalism; Methodism and Education; Christianity and Modern Unbelief; Indifferentism and Apathy; Methodist Literature; Methodist Young People's Societies; The Spiritual Vitality of Methodism; Family Religion and Worship; Temperance; Gambling; The Perils of Wealth; Pulpit Effectiveness; The Mobilization of the Church; and Foreign Missions.

The First Ecumenical Methodist Conference in 1881 had received the news of the assassination of President James A. Garfield, and there were appropriate addresses and resolutions. By an interesting coincidence this Third Conference received the news of the assassination of President William McKinley. The Rev. Dr. E. E. Jenkins of the Wesleyan Methodist Church, who twenty years before had moved the resolution concerning the death of Garfield, was one of the speakers who spoke concerning the attack on President McKinley. Most of the morning of September 7, 1901, after the attack on the President and before he had actually died, was occupied with a dozen statements concerning the tragedy and cablegrams were dispatched to the President, to Mrs. McKinley, and to John Hay, the American Secretary of State. There was a Memorial Service after the President's death.

Fourth Ecumenical Methodist Conference—1911

The Fourth Ecumenical Methodist Conference was held October 4-17, 1911, at the Metropolitan Methodist Church, Toronto, Canada. The published Proceedings show that the organization and routine which had been followed in the previous Conferences prevailed in this meeting. Of the total membership of five hundred, three hundred were assigned to the Western Section and two hundred to the Eastern Section, and the rules provided that so far as possible there should be an equal number of ministers and laymen. The Rules and Regulations did not differ greatly from those previously adopted, and the now familiar device of the four divisions and the selection of a secretary from each was continued.

The Chief Secretary was the Rev. H. K. Carroll, LL.D., of the Methodist Episcopal Church; and the others were the Rev. James Chapman, D.D., of the Wesleyan Methodist Church; Bishop C. H. Phillips, D. D., of the Colored Methodist Episcopal Church; and Alderman Thomas Snape, J. P., of the United Methodist Church. Thirty presidents representing the various participating churches were selected by the business committee. In addition to the bodies which had sent representatives to previous Conferences, delegates came to Toronto from the newly-formed Japan Methodist Church and the Methodist Church of New Zealand.

The Conference received a message from His Royal Highness, Field Marshal the Duke of Connaught, the Governor-General of Canada, to which it returned a message of thanks. A function was given by His Honor, the Lieutenant Governor, His Worship, the Mayor, and the City Council. The Methodist Social Union of Toronto gave a banquet for the Conference, and honorary degrees were conferred upon representatives of the different Methodist churches by Victoria University.

At this Conference the Methodist Historical Union was formed. It was a historical body coextensive with ecumenical Methodism, divided into Eastern and Western Sections, with headquarters in New York and London. The officers for the Eastern Section were the Rev. Frederick L. Wiseman, President; and the Rev. J. Alfred Sharp, Secretary and Treasurer. The Western officers were Bishop E. R. Hendrix, President; and Dr. H. K. Carroll, Secretary and Treasurer.

The program at Toronto followed in general those of the previous Conferences. There were reviews of the progress made in the various Sections during the decade, and Methodist ecumenicity, history, evangelism, missions, and education were covered by the addresses. The relation of the Church to social problems was brought forward more prominently; and there were addresses dealing with industry and commerce, the needs of modern life, international relations and world peace, socialism, settlement work, divorce, and the problem of the city church. An entire day was devoted to the subject of Temperance, and American prohibition was discussed at considerable length. A new awareness was discernible in essays and addresses on "The Psychology of Child Training," "The Equipment of the Sunday School Teacher," "Condition and Needs of Young People's Societies," and "The Church and the Recreation of Young People."

In this Conference the work and position of the women in the

Church was lifted up, and a session was devoted thereto. The topic was "Woman's Claims and Responsibilities." Among the women who participated were Mrs. W. I. Haven of the Methodist Episcopal Church, who presided; Mrs. Katherine Lent Stevenson of the Methodist Episcopal Church, who conducted the devotional services in the absence of Miss Clementina Butler, famous missionary to India; Mrs. Joseph Johnson of the Primitive Methodist Church; Mrs. T. J. Copeland of the Methodist Episcopal Church, South, who spoke in the absence of Miss Belle Bennett, noted American missionary leader; Mrs. Lucy Rider Meyer of the Methodist Episcopal Church, who discussed "Deaconesses and Sisterhoods"; Mrs. J. O. Robinson, whose name was later to be given to the outstanding Methodist school in Puerto Rico; and outstanding women leaders from the other Churches.

For the first time world Methodist statistics were presented to the Conference. These showed 48,614 ministers, 67,438 churches, and 7,409,736 members in the Western Section, while the churches of the Eastern Section reported 7,194 ministers, 32,059 churches, and 1,358,880 members. The total membership was, therefore, 8,768,616, which was a gain of 1,109,337 for the decade. The "Estimate of Methodist Population," or the total Methodist community or constituency throughout the world, was 32,728,574. This was the first attempt to estimate the total number of Methodist adherents throughout the world. For the Eastern Section it was based on the ratio of four adherents to each member, the number of members being multiplied by five; and for the Western Section it was based on the ratio of $2\frac{1}{2}$ adherents to each member, the number of members being multiplied by $3\frac{1}{2}$.

An interesting section of these statistics related to the giving of the Churches for the foreign missionary enterprise. The average of such giving per member for the foreign Churches of the Wesleyan Methodist Missionary Society was $6.50 per annum, this being the highest. The report from South Africa was $4.13 per member and that of the foreign Churches of the Methodist Episcopal Church was $2.37 per member. However, the Wesleyan Methodists of Great Britain and Ireland gave only $1.59 per member, and the home churches of the Methodist Episcopal Church gave sixty-three cents per member. The giving of world-wide Methodism for foreign missions averaged eighty cents per member per annum.

The preparation of these statistics was doubtless due to the work of Dr. H. K. Carroll, the Secretary-in-Chief, who was an American Methodist statistician and compiler of great ability. It was probably due also to Dr. Carroll's enterprise that the records of the closing session were actually read in printed form before the session adjourned.

The Fifth Ecumenical Methodist Conference—1921

The Fifth Ecumenical Methodist Conference met again in Wesley's Chapel on City Road in London on September 6, 1921, and continued through September 16. The opening service was conducted by the President of the Wesleyan Methodist Conference, the Rev. J. Arthur Sharp, who presented letters of greetings from the Archbishop of Canterbury and Mr. Lloyd George, the British Prime Minister. The official sermon was preached by the Rev. S. P. Rose, D.D., President of the Wesleyan College at Montreal.

The regulations under which this Conference was conducted were similar to those of the previous Conferences. Twenty-two presiding officers were selected for the various sessions by the business committee. The four secretaries chosen from the four divisions were the Rev. Dr. Herbert B. Workman of the Wesleyan Methodist Church, Mr. William S. Welch of the United Methodist Church, the Rev. Dr. H. K. Carroll of the Methodist Episcopal Church, and Mr. Oscar W. Adams of the African Methodist Episcopal Zion Church. The apportionment of delegates to the Eastern Section was 220, and 330 were allotted to the Western Section. In these allotments appeared for the first time definite representatives of foreign missions, fourteen to the Wesleyan Methodist Church, three to the

Primitive Methodist Church, three to the United Methodist Church, and thirty to the Western Section.

World War I had been waged since the previous Conference, and the world had not recovered from the war. Transportation rates were so high that many delegates were unable to attend, and the cost for those from Australia and New Zealand were nearly prohibitive. London was so crowded that housing was secured only with great difficulty and much effort. None of the previous Conferences had faced such handicaps as those encountered by the Fifth Session. It was, nevertheless, carried through successfully.

The program did not show great variation from those of the previous Conferences. The topics discussed were as follows: Ecumenical Methodism; The Position and Prospects of Evangelical Religion; Christian Unity; Interracial Brotherhood; Foreign Missions; World Peace; Women's Work; The Church and Youth; The Attitude of the People Toward Religion; Religious Journalism; Social and Industrial Problems; and, finally, the Lessons of the Conference. Of course, these general topics were broken down into various titles for the individual addresses.

The Conference sent a telegram of greeting to the newly-created League of Nations and received a reply from the Secretary General, who stated that the Conference's message had been published in the Assembly Journal. The United States had refused to join the League, which was regarded by some of the delegates as a political question in America. One speaker expressed the fear that in calling the Washington Conference the United States might set up a rival organization. These considerations had the effect of toning down to a certain degree the discussion concerning the League.

The business committee presented a report concerning the movement to erect a bronze equestrian statue of Bishop Francis Asbury in Washington, D.C., and this called forth enthusiastic comments. Concerning the work of Asbury, the American Secretary pointed out that the movement for such a monument was inaugurated at the Ecumenical Methodist Conference held in Toronto ten years previously and that it therefore represented World Methodism and not that of the United States only. He pointed out that Congress had set aside a site for the monument and expressed the hope that the Methodists of America and elsewhere would provide the remaining amount needed in order that the monument could be dedicated at an early day.

On the morning of September 13, Bishop W. N. Ainsworth of the Methodist Episcopal Church, South, proposed a resolution to the effect "that the conditions require the appointment of a Continuation Committee to conserve the results of this Ecumenical Conference, and for the furtherance of Methodism throughout the world; and that a Committee of 48 be appointed, 24 of the Eastern, and 24 of the Western Section." This was agreed to, and the Committee was appointed. In a later session Dr. Workman stated that the Continuation Committee desired to be called the Ecumenical Methodist Committee. There was a very keen desire, he stated, that the two Sections should be kept together as much as possible so that they might know more of each other and in the event of any crisis might speak with a united voice. "We shall try in the next ten years," he continued, "to be a very live body."

This Committee represented the first steps of World Methodism toward the formation of a permanent organization. Two conveners were designated but no officers were named. Nevertheless, it indicated a felt need and foreshadowed the organization which would have its beginnings a quarter of a century later. Because of its importance, the full action of the Committee should be printed herein:

"Be it resolved that it is the sense of this Committee that the conditions require the appointment of a Continuation Committee, to be entitled 'Ecumenical Methodist Committee,' to conserve the results of this Ecumenical Conference and represent it in the interim in the furtherance of Methodism throughout the world.

"Resolved that we appoint a committee of 48,—24 from the Eastern and 24 from the Western Section.

"Resolved that we ask approval of these nominations by the constituent bodies which they represent.

Ecumenical Methodist Committee

Western Section	*Eastern Section*
Rev. S. D. Chown, D.D.	Rev. J. A. Sharp
Rev. T. Albert Moore, D.D.	Rev. Dr. Workman (Convener)
Hon. N. W. Rowell, LL.D.	Rev. J. E. Wakerley
Mr. A. E. Ames	Rev. F. L. Wiseman
Bishop W. F. McDowell	Rev. W. Bardsley Brash
Bishop F. D. Leete, LL.D.	Rev. F. H. Benson
Dr. H. K. Carroll	Sir R. W. Perks, Bart.
Dr. Jas. R. Joy	Sir William Middlebrook
Hon. James Watson	Sir J. Barnsley
Bishop Edgar Blake, LL.D.	Rt. Hon. W. Runciman
Rev. D. G. Downey, LL.D.	Mr. G. Knight
Bishop J. W. Hamilton, LL.D.	Mr. I. H. Holden
(Convener)	Miss Lena Wallis
Hon. E. L. Kidney	Rev. Col. A. T. Holden, B.A.
Rev. Clarence True Wilson	(Australia)
Bishop W. N. Ainsworth, LL.D.	Rev. Charles S. Lucas (South
Bishop E. D. Mouzon, D.D.	Africa)
Rev. A. J. Weeks, D.D.	Rev. S. Horton
Rev. Thomas D. Ellis, D.D.	Rev. G. Armitage
Rev. H. A. Boaz, D.D.	Rev. J. T. Barkby
Hon. Josephus Daniels	Rev. A. Baldwin
Rev. T. H. Lewis, LL.D.	Dr. A. S. Peake
Bishop L. J. Coppin	Mr. H. H. Bowyer
Bishop C. H. Phillips	Mrs. Proud
Bishop J. S. Caldwell	Rev. W. Treffry
Mrs. J. H. McCoy	Rev. Dr. D. Brook
Mrs. Lovell	Rev. T. Sunderland
Mrs. M. R. Woodruffe	Sir R. Walter Essex
Bishop Pearce	Mr. Wm. S. Welch
Rev. Paul Barnhart	Mr. Wm. Mallinson, J.P.
	Mrs. Butler

"The Constituent Bodies be authorized to supply any vacancies.

Meetings of the Committee

"(1) That a meeting should be held three times in the decade, the last meeting to be one year before the next Ecumenical Conference.

"(2) Members of the Committee, if in the other country, to be entitled to be present.

"(3) That at least a quarterly letter be exchanged; and a Press Committee on each side be constituted to consider how best to get into touch and to exchange mutual information.

Matters Referred to the Committee

"(1) The question of *publicity*, including the question of how to secure better publicity for Methodist religious work, was referred to the Eastern Section at its first meeting of the Committee.

"(2) *Wesley at Lincoln College.*—The question of a Memorial Brass to Wesley at Lincoln College was referred to the Eastern Section of the Committee.

"(3) *Rhodes Scholars at Oxford.*—The Committee (Western Section) was also instructed to consider how best to obtain information of Methodist Rhodes Scholars attending Oxford, and their continued membership in the Methodist Church (see resolution below).

"(4) *Interchange of Pulpits between English and American Churches.* —This matter was referred to the favourable consideration of the Ecumenical Methodist Committee.

"(5) *Character and Arrangements of the next Ecumenical Conference.*—The Conference requested the Committee to consider the whole question of the character and arrangements of the next Ecumenical Conference, with power to act."

The Sixth Ecumenical Methodist Conference—1931

The Sixth Ecumenical Methodist Conference met in the Wesley Memorial Methodist Episcopal Church, South, in Atlanta, Georgia, on the evening of October 16, 1931, and continued through October 26. This Conference, according to the "rules and regulations," consisted of 220 delegates from the Eastern Section and 330 from the Western Section. The procedure in general was that which had been followed in all the previous Conferences, including the functioning of the business committee. The four divisions which had previously operated were eliminated, however, and the secretaries were nominated by the Eastern and Western Sections and elected by the Conference.

According to the rules adopted, the Chairman of the Program Committee of the Western Section should call the Conference to order at each general session and introduce the Chairman who had been chosen by the business committee. There were fifteen such presiding officers. The secretaries were the Rev. Herbert B. Workman, Litt. D., D.D., of the Wesleyan Methodist Church; Mr. James R. Joy, Litt. D., LL.D., of the Methodist Episcopal Church; and the Rev. Andrew J. Weeks, D.D., of the Methodist Episcopal Church, South. Dr. Joy was unable to attend the Conference, however, and the Rev. John M. Arters, D.D., of the Methodist Episcopal Church, was elected associate secretary to serve in his place.

This Conference set up four Discussion Groups. The officers of these groups and the topics discussed were as follows:

Group I—"Personal Religion." Chairman: Professor A. L. Humphries, M.A., Primitive Methodist Church; Secretary: The Rev. A. D. Porter, D.D., the Methodist Episcopal Church, South.

Group II—"Church Life." Chairman: Mr. John W. Barton, LL.D., Methodist Episcopal Church, South; Secretary: The Rev. W.H.B. Chapman, The United Methodist Church (England).

Group III—"Christian Social Order." Chairman: The Rev. Orien W. Fifer, D.D., Methodist Episcopal Church; Secretary: The Rev. William Corrigan, Methodist Church in Ireland.

Group IV—"Wider Human Relationships." Chairman: The Rev. Robert Bond, Wesleyan Methodist Church; Secretary: The Rev. John R. Edwards, D.D., Methodist Episcopal Church.

This Conference met during the world-wide business depression, and there was considerable uncertainty as to whether the meeting could be held. The City of Atlanta raised the necessary funds for local expenses, including the entertainment of all overseas delegates, and this action insured the success of the Conference. The city was chosen largely because John and Charles Wesley had lived and worked in Georgia, and on the last day the Conference made a pilgrimage to Savannah and visited the spots where the Wesleys and George Whitefield had worked in earlier days.

This was the first Ecumenical Conference which had a general theme for the whole program. The subject selected was "Methodism in the Life of Today." The approaching consummation of Methodist union in Great Britain was an important factor in the spirit and discussions of the Conference. Many of the subjects into which the general theme was subdivided were similar to those of other Conferences. There was, however, a new awareness of the contemporary situation in the fact that an entire session was devoted to "Religion and Science." The addresses were made by Professor William McDougall of Duke University, Professor Charles Felton Scott of Yale University, and Professor Arthur L. Foley of the Methodist Episcopal Church.

On Sunday, October 18, there were no general meetings of the Conference. Delegates, however, preached in many of the churches of Georgia and the neighboring states, and in the afternoon there were three great mass meetings in Atlanta: a meeting for men was at the Wesley Memorial Church, the women met at Saint Mark Methodist Church, while the young people gathered in the First Methodist Church.

Another innovation was the holding of what were called Eastern Section Platform Meetings on two evenings. One of these was an address by the famous evangelist, Gypsy Smith of the Wesleyan Methodist Church. The other featured addresses by the Rev. E. B. Storr of the Primitive Methodist Church, and Mr. Arthur A. Richards and the Rev. W. Harold Beals of the Wesleyan Methodist Church. On one evening a musical and dramatic spectacle entitled "Heaven Bound" was presented in the Atlanta auditorium by a group of 500 Negro singers.

Probably the outstanding feature of the program was an address on the afternoon of Sunday, October 21, by the President of the United States, Mr. Herbert Hoover; the President was not able to be present in person, but the Conference received his address by radio at the City Auditorium. Following the President's address, the Vice President of the United States, Mr. Charles Curtis, addressed the Conference in person.

Among the business matters which were brought before and adopted by the Conference was a resolution endorsing the commemoration of the sesquicentennial of the organization of American Methodism, which was held in Baltimore in 1934, the approval of the preparation of an Encyclopedia of Methodism, which was referred to the various Methodist Publishing Houses but which was never implemented, and a resolution expressing deep sympathy with the German Methodists in the difficulties which faced them and their nation in the light of the Treaty of Versailles.

This Sixth Ecumenical Methodist Conference made a still greater advance in the direction of a permanent form of organization. The Continuation Committee, which was set up in two Sections in 1921, had been able to do little except to plan for this Conference. At the present session this Ecumenical Methodist Committee was abandoned and for the first time an Ecumenical Council was set up. The importance of this action as preparing the way for the permanent organization adopted in 1951 deserves further consideration. What might be regarded as the constitution of this Ecumenical Methodist Council was as follows:

Ecumenical Council

The Council shall organize by the election of the following officers:
1. Two coordinate Presidents and two coordinate Secretaries, one of each from the Eastern Section and one of each from the Western Section, whose terms shall be determined by their respective sections. The two Presidents shall preside alternately at all convocations of the Council and the two Secretaries shall serve jointly. All announcements or Addresses to the Church by the Council shall be signed by these officers in their coordinate capacity unless otherwise ordered. These two Presidents and Secretaries shall be the President and the Secretary respectively of the Eastern and Western Sections.
2. Other than the President and Secretary provided above, the

Eastern and Western Sections shall organize themselves, with such Vice Presidents and Secretaries and a Treasurer as each shall determine for itself.

3. Each section shall be empowered to fill any vacancies in the Council officers that may occur *ad interim*.

4. There shall be an Executive Committee of ten members from the Council, five from the Eastern and five from the Western Section, to be elected by each Section, and in addition thereto the two Presidents and Secretaries and Treasurers shall be members *ex officio*.

5. The Executive Committee shall meet annually, if possible, and constitute a medium through which joint action may be secured on all matters pertaining to our common Ecumenical interests by the two sections. It shall provide for meetings of the Council when it is deemed necessary and practicable.

6. The Eastern and Western Sections shall meet annually and at such other times as each may deem necessary.

Pursuant to this plan and on nomination of the business committee and election by the Conference, the following officiary was set up:

Executive Committee, Western Section: Bishop F. D. Leete, Methodist Episcopal Church, President; Rev. A. J. Weeks, Methodist Episcopal Church, South, Secretary; Bishop W. N. Ainsworth, Methodist Episcopal Church, South; Rev. T. Albert Moore, United Church of Canada; Rev. Edmund D. Soper, Methodist Episcopal Church; Rev. J. C. Broomfield, Methodist Protestant Church; Bishop G. C. Clement, African Methodist Episcopal Zion Church.

Executive Committee, Eastern Section: Rev. F. Luke Wiseman, Wesleyan Methodist Church, President; Rev. H. B. Workman, Wesleyan Methodist Church, Secretary; Rev. Henry Smith, United Methodist Church; Rev. Samuel Horton, Wesleyan Methodist Church; Rev. E. Aldom French, Wesleyan Methodist Church; Rev. J. T. Barkby, Wesleyan Methodist Church; Mr. W. S. Welch, United Methodist Church.

The Conference furthermore adopted the following agenda for the first meeting of the Ecumenical Council:

Agenda—Ecumenical Council

In view of the fact that the sections of the Council will meet in separate countries, a common agenda is essential for the first meeting, the different sections to communicate their findings to one another after the first meeting.

1. To consider the work intrusted to the Council and the perfecting of its organization.

2. To consider the report of the Ecumenical Conference with a view to the use of its findings for the work of world Methodism.

3. To consider methods whereby the different Departments or Boards of the Methodist Churches dealing with the same subject may be brought into closer cooperation with one another.

(a) *Foreign Mission:* Especially with reference to the question raised in the Wesleyan Methodist Conference of Great Britain as to securing more regular communication between the Foreign Missionary Societies or Boards—closer cooperation in the field—and whether, in particular fields, special developments could be fostered.

(b) *Home Missions:* Especially as to an exchange of information with reference to new and effective developments of evangelistic methods, and as to the possibility of mutual help.

(c) *Temperance and Social Welfare:* Especially as to the securing of authoritative information with regard to the working of, and the effect of, such activities as prohibition and other efforts to control the liquor traffic; also as to what methods could be adopted for the raising of standards of the cinema and the suppression of gambling and prize fighting.

4. What steps can be taken by world Methodism for the prevention of war and the establishment of permanent peace.

5. Suggestions for the next meeting of the Council and any other business.

The Seventh Ecumenical Methodist Conference—1947

The Ecumenical Methodist Conference had been greatly handicapped in 1921 by World War I and in 1931 by the world-wide economic depression. Worse was to follow, however, for the Conference scheduled for 1941 was wholly prevented by World War II, which was raging at the time. Not until 1947 was it possible to bring the Conference together, and on this occasion it was attended by the smallest number of delegates from the churches other than those of the Americas that had ever attended any of the preceding Conferences. In spite of this fact, however, the Seventh Conference was one of the most important ever held from the standpoint of its actions and their results.

The Conference was held in the Trinity Methodist Church at Springfield, Massachusetts, U.S.A., September 24-October 2, 1947. British Methodism was represented by 45 delegates, including six wives of the delegates. From the rest of the world outside the United States came 39 delegates. The Methodist churches of the United States were represented by more than 350 representatives. Thus the Americans outnumbered the rest of the world more than four to one because of the restrictions on both travel and finances produced by the war.

The program, of course, was of a high order since the leaders of world Methodism were present. The Rev. Dr. Wilbert F. Howard of the British Methodist Church had been elected Chairman of the Eastern Section; and Bishop Ivan Lee Holt of The Methodist Church, U.S.A., was Chairman of the Western Section. These Chairmen presided at all the sessions of the Conference. The entire day of Thursday, September 25, was devoted to a review of Methodism during the sixteen years which had elapsed since the last Conference, the various speakers presenting surveys from Great Britain, Australia, South Africa, Latin America, Asia, and the United States. Further addresses on social tensions, the witness of Methodism, Methodism's responsibility in the redemption of society, and Methodism and the larger fellowship were all influenced by the world situation which the great war had created.

At this Conference it was found that the Methodist Historical Union which had been formed at Toronto in 1911 had not functioned. An ecumenical body was formed under the name of the International Methodist Historical Society, of which Bishop Paul N. Garber, then residing in Geneva, Switzerland, was elected President;

and the Rev. Frank Baker of Great Britain and Dr. Elmer T. Clark of the United States were elected Secretaries.

At Springfield another great advance was made in the discussion of a permanent organization. The Committee on Reorganization secured the adoption of its report by which the Ecumenical Methodist Conference was completely reorganized. The two-section arrangement with officers from each was continued until the next Ecumenical Conference in order to avoid a sudden break with the past. The modern arrangement by which the Council was divided into Sections representing the various areas of the world was set up, and 24 such sections with a membership of 226 were formed to give representation to all Methodist bodies in the world.

This Conference also provided that the Conference should in the future meet at five year intervals, and an Executive Committee was created for *ad interim* meetings.

For the first time provision was made for certain standing committees. These were: (1) The Committee on Exchange of Ministers; (2) The Committee on International Affairs to cooperate with the World Council of Churches; (3) A Committee on Woman's Work, a constitution for which was placed in the hands of a Continuation Committee; (4) A Committee on Young People's Work; (5) A Committee on Evangelism, and (6) A Committee on Finances.

The following officers of the reorganized Ecumenical Methodist Council were elected, the first name in each case being that of an American and the second that of a British Methodist:

Chairmen: Bishop Ivan Lee Holt, Rev. Dr. Wilbert F. Howard.

Vice-Chairmen: Bishop Paul N. Garber, Mr. A. Victor Murray.

Secretaries: Rev. Dr. Oscar Thomas Olson, Rev. Dr. Harold Roberts.

Treasurers: Dr. M. S. Davage, Rev. Dr. Benjamin Gregory.

The Eighth Ecumenical Methodist Conference—1951

The Eighth Ecumenical Methodist Conference met at Oxford in England on August 28-September 7, 1951. The world had attained to a more nearly stable status, and most of the Sections of the world were again represented. In fact, only one of the 24 Sections failed to send its delegates. The official membership was, therefore, about 225; but provision had been made for delegates and official visitors which put the actual attendance considerably above 1,000. Several companies of tourists from America arranged their itineraries by way of Oxford to enable their participants to spend at least a short time at the Conference.

In view of the discussions of the preceding Conferences, it seems unnecessary to discuss here the nature of the program and the topics for the numerous addresses. The Executive Committee met in advance in London; and a great pre-conference public meeting was held at the Central Hall, Westminster, on the night of August 27. There was a meeting of welcome in the Sheldonean Theatre at Oxford on the evening of August 28, to which the delegates were welcomed by the Bishop of Manchester, the Moderator of the Free Church Federation Council, the Methodists of Oxford, and His Majesty, The King. The daily sessions were held in the Wesley Memorial Church at Oxford.

One of the significant items of business was the unanimously favorable action taken by the Conference on the report of the International Methodist Historical Society which had been formed at Springfield in 1947. This report contained the Constitution of the Society, and officers of the Society were elected. The most significant item of business, however, was the adoption of a policy which included the preparation and publication of the following works: (1) *Who's Who in Methodism*; (2) *An Album of Methodist History*; (3) *An Annotated Edition of the Journal and Letters of Francis Asbury*; (4) *An Encyclopedia of Methodism*.

A committee was set up to consider the establishment of an

Oxford Memorial to John and Charles Wesley to take the form of a World Methodist Center with provisions for forty or more resident students.

There were reports from the Committee on Woman's Work, the Youth Committee, and the Committee on Faith and Order.

One of the most important actions of this Conference was the launching of the World Mission of Evangelism. This was carried out under the direction of the Committee on Evangelism, of which the Rev. Dr. W. E. Sangster of London was Chairman, and was participated in by many of the Sections in various parts of the world. Notable results were achieved in Great Britain, the United States, Australia, and elsewhere. This was the first simultaneous movement in which the Methodists of the world had participated since the days of John Wesley.

At the Oxford Conference the following standing committees were set up: Finance; Evangelism; Exchange of Preachers; Oxford Memorial; Woman's Work; Education; Youth and Adult Work; Faith and Order. The last named committee was in two sections, a Church Relations Section and a Theological Section.

This Conference provided for the drafting of a permanent Constitution to be submitted for adoption in 1956. It also perfected a permanent organization. The East-West sectional arrangement was dropped, and a Permanent Secretariat was elected. A General Executive Committee was set up, and similar committees were organized for Great Britain and the United States of America.

After Oxford: 1951-1956

To round out this survey a word should be said concerning the activities of the World Methodist Council between the Oxford and Lake Junaluska Conferences. The administration set up in 1951 was expected to develop a fully functioning organization, and the Secretaries to all intents and purposes devoted their full time to the work. Headquarters were established at Birmingham in England, and at Lake Junaluska and New York in the United States. For the first time the Council assumed the form of a permanently organized and staffed body, with financial support provided by the British Conference and the General Conference of The Methodist Church, U.S.A. The Executive Committee met annually, twice in the United States, once in England, and once in Ireland. At its meeting at Birmingham, England, in 1953, it was decided to hold the Ninth World Methodist Conference at Lake Junaluska in 1956.

Progress was made in developing contacts between the various Sections of the Council. Biennial conferences of British and European Methodists were held on the Continent. Officers from the United States visited the Methodists of the West Indies, Australia, New Zealand, and other parts of the world, and the Chairman of the Committee on Evangelism visited Asia and the South Pacific area as the representative of the World Methodist Council in connection with other duties.

The editorial and publication policy adopted at Oxford on the recommendation of the affiliated historical group was implemented by the American Association of Methodist Historical Societies under the editorial supervision of the Secretary in the United States. *Who's Who in Methodism* and *An Album of Methodist History* were both published in 1952. The *Annotated Edition of the Journal and Letters of Francis Asbury* has been practically completed and will be published jointly by the Epworth Press of Great Britain and the Abingdon Press of the United States, the first work to appear under the imprint of both publishing houses. This work is under the sponsorship of the Historical Publications Commission of the United States Government as well as that of the World Methodist Council and the associated Methodist historical societies of the world, the highest auspices ever enjoyed by any Methodist project. It will be in three large volumes and should be ready late in 1956. In view of the labor involved in these productions it was not possible to do any work on the *Encyclopedia of Methodism*.

Of much importance in giving stability and permanence to the Council was the erection of a headquarters building at Lake Junaluska, U.S.A. This World Methodist Building, worth approximately $100,000, was erected with funds raised or given by the Bishops of The Methodist Church in its Southeastern Jurisdiction and other friends of the ecumenical movement on property donated by the Trustees of the Lake Junaluska Assembly. It is owned by the World Methodist Council which was incorporated in order to hold such property. The building contains the administrative and executive offices of the Council and the Association of Methodist Historical Societies, the considerable Wesleyana and Methodistica collection of the Secretary in the United States, and portraits of John Wesley, Francis Asbury, and the officers of the World Methodist Council executed by the celebrated Frank O. Salisbury of London.

The British Conference secured the Old Rectory at Epworth, boyhood home of John and Charles Wesley, for preservation and use as a shrine of Methodism, and at the Executive meeting in Belfast, Ireland, in 1955, resolutions were adopted providing for its acquisition and maintenance by the World Methodist Council. The Secretary in England also secured the adoption by the Corporation of West Bromwich of Asbury's boyhood home as a historical site, thus insuring its preservation.

All this indicates that after Oxford the World Methodist Council made considerable progress toward the goal of establishing itself as a permanent, recognized, and fully functioning administrative agency which will be able adequately to represent World Methodism among the other ecumenical bodies.

CHAPTER IX

THE METHODISTS OF THE WORLD

At the Eighth Ecumenical Conference held at Oxford, England, in 1951, a booklet was presented with the above title, in which was published brief historical sketches of the Methodist bodies of the world and statistics of their membership and constituency. This was later revised and reprinted in the *Handbook of Information* of the World Methodist Council and forms the basis for this statement.

Only independent Methodist bodies are here described. In Continental Europe, Asia, Africa, and the South Pacific area most Methodist work is related to the Methodist bodies in America, Great Britain, or Australasia, and therefore is not included in this section. Total world Methodism, by countries and by churches, is listed in the statistical survey in Chapter X.

Great Britain

The Methodist Church

The mother church of Ecumenical Methodism grew out of the Evangelical Revival of the eighteenth century, led by John Wesley (1703-1791) and Charles Wesley (1707-1788), aided by a host of other evangelists, ministerial and lay.

A group of young students, led by the two Wesley brothers, met for study and devotion and social service at Oxford from 1729 onwards. They were called in derision "The Holy Club," or "The Methodists." Around 1735 this group broke up as the Wesleys went as missionaries to Georgia, followed by their great collaborator, George Whitefield (1714-1770). During this period they came under the influence of the Moravians, and were eventually led by them to a personal experience of saving faith.

Methodism as we know it may be said to date from May 24, 1738, when John Wesley wrote in his *Journal*: "I felt my heart strangely warmed. I felt I did trust in Christ, Christ alone for salvation; and an assurance was given me that He had taken away *my* sins, even *mine,* and saved *me* from the law of sin and death." The Wesleys gathered around them others who sought or had found a similar experience, first in London, then in Bristol, and soon throughout England. In 1739 their first building was opened, the "New Room in the Horse Fair" in Bristol. Later in the same year the Foundery was acquired as their London headquarters, which was superseded in 1778 by Wesley's Chapel in City Road. In 1742 the first Class Meeting was organized at Bristol, and in 1744 the first Conference was held at the Foundery.

Significant events and dates are the following: (1) The organization of the Holy Club at Oxford in 1729; (2) The conversion of John Wesley at Aldersgate, 1738; (3) Beginning of field preaching, 1739; (4) The formation of a group in London, 1739; (5) The erection of the first chapel at Bristol, 1739; (6) The beginning of lay preaching, 1740 or 1741; (7) The first class meeting at Bristol, 1742; (8) The first conference in London, 1744.

The revival spread rapidly throughout the British Isles, particularly in the growing industrial area. Everywhere the converts and "seekers" were grouped together in Societies, for whom lay preachers and class leaders provided continuous guidance and pastoral oversight. The whole "Connexion" was linked together by John Wesley's organizing genius, while his brother Charles provided in his hymns both inspiration and a solid grounding in the faith. In 1784 Wesley drew up his Deed of Declaration, which gave Methodism status as a separate legal entity, and vested its control in the annual Conference.

After the death of the Wesleys various disagreements arose over matters of church government. These gave rise to several offshoots from the main body. Almost all these divisions were healed in 1932 by the union in the Methodist Church of Wesleyan Methodists, Primitive Methodists, and United Methodists. Two small groups, the Wesleyan Reform Union and the Independent Methodist Churches, remained outside the united body.

There are over 750,000 members of the Methodist Church in Great Britain, together with about 300,000 in its overseas missions. Over 8,000 churches and other preaching places are cared for by 4,500 ministers. From the beginning British Methodism has made large use of lay preachers, and at present there are over 25,000 of whom one-tenth are women.

Wesleyan Reform Union

The Wesleyan Reform Union dates back to a controversy over what the "Reformers" regarded as autocracy and abuses of power in the Wesleyan Conference. The expulsion of three ministers from the Conference in 1849 proved a rallying point for those who were dissatisfied, and during the following years many old societies broke away from Wesleyan Methodism, or groups broke away to form new Societies. In 1857 many of these came together with earlier small secessions to form the United Methodist Free Churches, while those remaining in 1859 took the name of the Wesleyan Reform Union, which has about 6,500 members in Great Britain.

Independent Methodist Churches

Very soon after Wesley's death a number of Methodist societies in the northwest developed their evangelistic zeal along their own lines. In particular they objected to the overriding power of the Conference, and to a separated ministry. These societies grouped themselves together under various names, but they have been known throughout most of a hundred and fifty years as Independent Methodists. They have approximately 8,000 members.

The Methodist Conference in Ireland

John Wesley made the first of his twenty-one visits to Ireland in 1747, finding 280 Methodists who had been gathered together in

Dublin by pioneer lay preachers. The work spread very rapidly inwards and served to strengthen the Protestant witness in that predominantly Roman Catholic country. The first chapel was opened at Dublin in 1752, and the first Conference was held at Limerick the same year. Emigrants from Ireland during the eighteenth and nineteenth centuries were of immense importance in spreading Methodism to other parts of the world. They included Barbara Heck, Philip Embury, Robert Strawbridge, and Robert Williams, pioneers in the United States of America, and Laurence Coughlan, the founder of Methodism in Newfoundland.

Wales

Welch Methodism forms a part of the British Conference, though maintaining a certain amount of self-government under it own Assembly. There are about 25,000 members. There was in Wales a parallel movement to the Evangelical Revival in England, which resulted in a body formerly known as the Calvinistic Methodist Church. This found its affinity with the Presbyterians rather than with the Methodists, however, and is now called the Presbyterian Church of Wales. It has approximately 175,000 members.

Continental Europe

Reference to the statistics in Chapter IX will show that nearly all the Methodist churches on the continent and in North Africa are now part of The Methodist Church of the United States. Relations have been disrupted in Hungary, Bulgaria, Yugoslavia, Czechoslovakia, Poland, Finland, and the Baltic States. Central and Southern Europe, North Africa, Germany, and Scandinavia are organized as Central Conferences with semi-autonomy. They elect their own bishops.

Italy

Methodism came to Italy in 1861, when the Wesleyan Missionary Society sent out two missionaries to support the evangelistic labors

THE METHODISTS OF THE WORLD

of an ex-priest, Bartolomeo Gualtieri of Florence. One of the missionaries, Henry J. Piggott, gave forty years of his life to Italian Methodism. American Methodism arrived in 1873, and organized many valuable forms of social service, though the only one remaining is the noted Casa Materna Orphanage in Naples. One of the great leaders of American Methodism in Italy was William Burt, elected to the episcopacy in 1904. After long years of close co-operation the British and American churches in Italy merged fully in 1946. There are at present probably 5,000 members.

France

Methodism entered France from England in 1791. The Methodist movement became the French Wesleyan Conference in 1852. The Methodist Episcopal Church of the United States began work in France in 1907, and greatly strengthened its programme after 1918. But French Methodism was unable to work out self-support; therefore the Conference was disbanded in 1935. The congregations in Alsace-Lorraine were attached to Switzerland, and most of the other Methodist congregations were merged with the French Reformed Church. Six groups remained, and there may be as many as 1,000 members in them.

United States of America
The Methodist Church

Methodist preaching in the United States was started almost simultaneously by Robert Strawbridge in Maryland and Philip Embury in New York. Priority between the two societies remains a moot question. But Embury's work began in 1766, and some competent historians assign an even earlier date to the preaching of Strawbridge. Both of these men were Methodist immigrants from Ireland. Strawbridge built a meetinghouse on Sam's Creek soon after his arrival in Maryland, and the first church was built in New York in 1769.

Mr. Wesley sent Richard Boardman and Joseph Pilmoor to

America in 1769, and during the following years ten other missionaries went out from the British Isles. One of these was Francis Asbury, who was sent in 1771. He became the leader of the Methodists, the greatest of all the "circuit riders," and the virtual father of American Methodism; and under his leadership the movement spread rapidly over the country, outstripping all other churches in growth.

The organization of American Methodism into an independent church on an episcopal basis was the result of Wesley's action in ordaining ministers for America and "consecrating" or "setting apart," by the imposition of hands, Dr. Thomas Coke as "superintendent" for the American work. At the Christmas Conference held in Baltimore in 1784, the Methodist Episcopal Church was formed, Francis Asbury being elected superintendent or bishop and duly consecrated by Coke, assisted by other ministers.

In the course of time there were numerous splits in American Methodism. The Methodist Protestant Church drew away in 1830, abolishing episcopacy and admitting laymen to the conferences. In 1844 the General Conference reached an impasse over the question of slavery and adopted a Plan of Separation under which the southern conferences organized the Methodist Episcopal Church, South. These three bodies united in 1939 to form The Methodist Church.

The Methodist Church is the largest Protestant body in America. In 1955 it reported over 10,000,000 members in 40,000 preaching places, with 42,373 ministers of all grades. Its property was valued at more than $1,335,000,000, and its annual expenditures for all purposes was nearly $250,000,000.

The church has over 20 administrative boards and agencies. Its missionary work is in fifty countries, and there are 5,000 churches and nearly a million members in its foreign fields. It operates 150 institutions of learning in the United States, including 9 universities, 10 theological seminaries, 69 colleges, 24 junior colleges, 8 academies, 1 professional school, and 30 schools of a missionary nature. These enroll nearly 225,000 students; their properties are valued at $200,000,000, and their endowment funds total above $242,600,000. There are 74 Methodist hospitals and 178 homes for children of all ages in the United States; and these care for nearly 1,500,000 persons each year and have properties worth $185,000,000.

African Methodist Episcopal Church

This is the second largest Methodist body in America, and the largest Negro Methodist group. It originated in 1787 when a group of Negro Methodists in Philadelphia withdrew from the Methodist Episcopal Church and built a chapel of their own. In 1799 Bishop Asbury ordained the Rev. Richard Allen, and in 1816 he led in the organization of an independent church. The body has flourished and now has 7,500 churches and more than a million members. It operates 17 educational institutions and has missionary work in Africa and the West Indies.

African Methodist Episcopal Zion Church

This third largest Methodist group in America dates from 1796 when Negro members left John Street Church in New York. In 1800 they built a chapel called Zion, and took the name of African Methodist Episcopal Church. The white church provided a ministry for several years. But an independent general conference was convened in 1921, and the name of the chapel was added to the name of the Church. A white bishop presided at this conference, and James Varrick was elected the first bishop of the new Church. The body has grown and now has over 2,000 churches and 525,000 members. It has six educational institutions and several foreign missions.

African Union First Colored Methodist Protestant Church

This is a Methodist Protestant body organized in 1866. It has around 40 churches and 2,500 members.

Apostolic Methodist Church

This is a very small body of the "fundamentalist" type which was organized in Florida in 1932. It has only two or three churches and fewer than 100 members.

Christian Methodist Church

In 1870 the Negro members of the Methodist Episcopal Church, South, asked to be set up as an independent church. The Colored Methodist Episcopal Church was accordingly organized. It was always regarded as a sister church of the southern denomination and sustains the same relation to The Methodist Church. It is one of the large Negro Methodist churches, having more than 4,000 churches and 385,000 members. It operates five institutions of learning. In 1956 it changed its name to Christian Methodist Church.

Colored Methodist Protestant Church

This is a one-congregation remnant of a group formed in Maryland in 1840. It has about 200 members.

Congregational Methodist Church

Formed in 1852 by certain persons in Georgia who withdrew from the Methodist Episcopal Church, South, in a dispute over episcopacy. It has about 160 churches and 11,000 members.

Congregational Methodist Church of U.S.A., Inc.

A small body organized at Forsyth, Georgia, in 1852. It now has about 100 churches and 6,000 members.

Evangelical Methodist Church

This body grew out of a protest at what its organizers regarded as a departure from Methodist doctrine in 1946. It is conservative and congregational and has about 50 churches and 5,000 members.

Free Methodist Church

The Free Methodist Church is an outgrowth of the controversy over holiness or Christian perfection. It was organized in 1860 under the leadership of the Rev. B. T. Robert and the Rev. Joseph Mc-Creary, who with others were expelled from the Genesee Conference in the heat of the dispute. It adheres to the holiness tradition and is conservative in nature. The church has about 1,200 congregations, 50,000 members, several institutions, and missions in Africa, India, Japan, China, and the Dominican Republic. It is episcopal in nature and has headquarters at Winona Lake, Indiana.

Holiness Methodist Church

A small body organized at Forest City, North Carolina, in 1913. It was previously known as the Lumber River Conference and represented a defection from the Wesleyan Methodist Church. It has about half-a-dozen churches and fewer than 1,000 members.

Independent African Methodist Episcopal Church

This body was formed by twelve ministers of the African Methodist Church who withdrew in 1907 after a dispute with district superintendents at Jacksonville, Florida. It has a dozen churches and about 1,000 members.

New Congregational Methodist Church

A small body with two dozen churches and 1,500 members in Georgia and Florida. It grew out of a dispute concerning the consolidation of certain rural churches in Georgia in 1881. Foot washing is practiced and episcopacy is rejected.

People's Methodist Church

A conservative holiness body which left The Methodist Church in North Carolina in 1939. It has about 25 congregations with perhaps 1,000 members and a Bible school at Greensboro, N.C.

Primitive Methodist Church

This church is an importation from England in 1829, where the parent body was formed in 1812 as a result of the labors of the spectacular American "camp meeting" evangelist, Lorenzo Dow.

It has about 90 churches and 12,000 members and supports a mission in Guatemala.

Reformed Methodist Church

A body which originated in Vermont in 1814. It grew out of the controversy over episcopacy and holiness, the new group retaining the latter. It flourished for a period, but there are now only a dozen churches and fewer than 500 members in the country.

Reformed Methodist Union Episcopal Church

Organized at Charleston, South Carolina, in 1885 by ministers and members who withdrew from the African Methodist Church in a dispute over the election of delegates to the General Conference. It adopted episcopacy in 1896, its first bishop being consecrated in 1899 by a bishop of the Reformed Episcopal Church. It has about two dozen churches and 1,000 members.

Reformed New Congregational Methodist Church

A small conservative body formed in Illinois in 1916 by an evangelist of the Congregational Methodist Church. It opposes divorce, secret societies, and personal adornment. It has eight congregations with around 500 members.

Reformed Zion Union Apostolic Church

Organized in Virginia in 1869 by a minister of the African Methodist Zion Church. It was originally called Zion Union Apostolic Church. There are about 50 churches and 20,000 members.

Southern Methodist Church

This body is composed of a few conservative churches, mainly in South Carolina and Georgia, which rejected Methodist unification in 1939. It has about 40 small congregations and 6,000 members.

Union American Methodist Episcopal Church

Organized in 1813 and composed of a group of Negroes who withdrew from Asbury Church at Wilmington, Delaware, in 1805.

It was first called the Union Church of Africans. The present name dates from a split in 1850 over lay representation in the conferences. There are 70 churches and about 10,000 members.

Wesleyan Methodist Church

This body orginally grew out of the controversy over slavery. It was formed in 1843 by a group of abolitionists; and when the slavery issue was settled by emancipation, it continued to attract adherents because of its conservative nature and its emphasis on Christian perfection. It has 900 churches, 38,000 members, 4 schools, and missions in Africa, India, and Japan.

Canada

United Church of Canada

Methodism was established in Canada as early as 1765 by Laurence Coughlan, one of Wesley's preachers, who went from Ireland to Newfoundland. William Black, "The Apostle of Nova Scotia," began preaching in 1779. The various branches of Methodism in England and the United States in due course established themselves, but in 1884 these were all united to form the Methodist Church in Canada. Unification was thus achieved in Canada 48 years before the union in Great Britain and 55 years before the merger in the United States.

The United Church of Canada, product of the union in 1925 of the Methodist, Presbyterian, and Congregational Churches, is the inheritor of the Wesleyan tradition and a member of the Ecumenical Methodist Council. At the time of the merger the Methodists constituted the strongest religious group in the Dominion, and they brought into the United Church 4,107 churches, 418,352 members, and 329 colleges, schools, and institutions.

The United Church of Canada is non-episcopal in character. The body now has 6,500 congregations, 3,500 ministers, and 870,000 church members. Its church and parsonage buildings are worth $126,000,000, and it raises $21,000,000 annually for its work.

131

Latin America

Methodist Church of Brazil

The first Methodist preachers went to Brazil in 1835 but accomplished little. Churches were established by the Methodist Episcopal Church, South (U.S.A.), in 1871, and thereafter there was steady growth. In 1930 the Methodist Church of Brazil was organized as an independent body, related to American Methodism as an affiliated autonomous church. The Church has 3 conferences, 3 bishops, 235 churches with 40,000 members. It has a publishing house which issues four periodicals, and 16 institutions with an enrollment of nearly 10,000 students.

Methodist Church of Mexico

Methodism was established in Mexico in 1871 and 1873 by the two large Methodist bodies of the United States. In 1930 all the work was united to form the independent Methodist Church of Mexico, which is related to The Methodist Church in the United States as an affiliated autonomous church.

The Methodist Church of Mexico has 75 ministers, 140 churches, and around 37,000 members. It is episcopal in character. The principal institutions are a publishing house, a Union Theological Seminary, a hospital, four social centers, and ten schools of secondary grade.

Africa

Methodist Church of South Africa

Methodists from Great Britain were in South Africa as early as 1806, and in 1816 Barnabas Shaw went out as a missionary. In 1883 South African Methodism was organized under its own conference, which was enlarged by Methodist Union. By Act of Parliament the independent Methodist Church of South Africa was constituted in 1927. This body now has more than 6,500 churches, 400 ordained preachers, 460 evangelists, and 11,000 local or lay preachers. Its total membership, including junior members and those on trial, is nearly 550,000. Its ministers are trained at theological colleges attached to Rhodes University at Grahamstown and at South African Native College at Fort Hare. The other outstanding institutions are Kingswood College for Boys at Grahamstown, Kearnsey College for Boys at Botha's Hill in Natal, Epworth High School for Girls at Pietermaritzburg, and Wesley Training College for Colored Methodists at Salt River. Fourteen African Training, Industrial, and Secondary high schools are operated; and there are 12 African rural secondary day schools. Other institutions include 3 missionary hospitals, 7 children's homes and orphanages, a publishing house and two book depots, and an influential newspaper, the *South African Weekly*, published at Johannesburg.

Methodist Church of West Africa

The Methodist Church of West Africa is an independent body in Sierra Leone. It was formed in 1934 or 1935 as the result of a secession from the former United Methodist Church following frictions after the union of British Methodism in 1932. It is an all-African body which has not spread far beyond the area around Freetown. It has about 3,000 members.

Asia

United Church of Christ in Japan

American and Canadian Methodists began working in Japan in 1873. The work flourished to such an extent that all Methodist bodies united in 1907 to form the independent Japan Methodist Church on an episcopal basis. In 1940 this body joined the *Kyodan* or United Church of Christ in Japan, and Methodism thus disappeared as a separate entity. At that time the Japan Methodist Church had 500 churches, 225 ordained preachers, 108 Bible women, and 30,000 members. It maintained 17 institutions of learning with over 20,000 students.

Korean Methodist Church

The Methodist Episcopal Church entered Korea in 1884 and the Methodist Episcopal Church, South, followed in 1895. The two American denominations united their work in 1930 to form the independent Korean Methodist Church. At the beginning of the war in 1939 this body had 867 churches and preaching places with 23,730 members and probationers. There was also a mission in Manchuria which had 24 churches and 4,225 adherents. The Church was subjected to much pressure during the war and at its close there were splits, but these were healed and the Church was reunited. The war between North and South Korea disrupted the work and destroyed much of the property, but it was in due course restored. It has around 62,000 members.

Church of South India

On September 27, 1947, the formal inauguration of the Church of South India brought into one body Methodists, Presbyterians, and Anglicans. The Church, which is episcopal in government, maintains fraternal relations with the World Methodist Council, because nearly a quarter of a million Methodists went into the new body. The united Church has 5,260 preaching places, 245,000 members, and a total constituency of 845,000. Of these totals the contribution of British Methodism was 1,560 congregations, including baptized adherents. In this Methodist community were 1,300 Sunday schools with 36,000 scholars, 1,100 elementary day schools with 43,000 students enrolled, and an extensive medical work.

South Pacific

Methodist Church of Australasia

The first Methodist class in Australia met in the home of Thomas Bowden, a layman, on March 6, 1812. On August 10, 1815, the Rev. Samuel Leigh arrived under the auspices of the Wesleyan Missionary Society in London, and he was joined in 1818 by the Rev. Walter Lawry. These two missionaries, and especially Leigh, are regarded as the fathers of Methodism in the South Pacific area. The first Methodist church building south of the equator was erected near Sydney about 1820. In 1855 Wesleyan Methodism throughout the continent was organized under an independent conference, which met for the first time in Sydney. Gradually the work was subdivided between five separate Australian Conferences, New Zealand also becoming separated in 1910. All the major Methodist denominations of Great Britain emigrated to Australasia, but united before their parent bodies in the mother country.

The Australian Church has 923 ordained ministers, 3,336 local or lay preachers, 2,656 churches, and around 350,000 members. The census reports 1,000,000 avowed adherents.

The Overseas Mission Board has stations in many lands of the South Pacific. There are over 200,000 members in its mission churches. The chief island missions are Fiji, Samoa, Papua, New Guinea, and Tonga.

Methodist Church of New Zealand

The Rev. Samuel Leigh went from Australia to New Zealand in 1821 and preached the first Methodist sermon to the Maoris. The Rev. Walter Lawry became superintendent of the New Zealand mission in 1844, and proved a wise administrator.

The first New Zealand Conference met in 1874, and the next year it was represented in the Australasian Conference. The Australian Church approved the separation of New Zealand in 1910, and the Methodist Church of New Zealand was formally set up by parliamentary action. Various Methodist bodies in Great Britain had established missions in New Zealand, and these were united in 1913.

In the New Zealand Methodist Church there are 436 churches and 342 other preaching places. There are 640 local preachers and 217 ordained ministers. The church adherents number 156,000, according to the government census. The churches report a smaller number of actual members, about 38,000. The foreign missions are in the Solomon Islands, with Bougainville and Buka on New Guinea.

CHAPTER X

THE WORLD METHODIST COMMUNITY

Many, perhaps most, church bodies report adherents loosely by families, racial or ethnic status, or even total populations. This is true of Roman Catholic, Jewish, and state-related groups. The method results in more or less extravagant claims which disparage the strength and influence of the Methodist and other free evangelical churches.

The Secretaries of the World Methodist Council in 1954 were instructed "to contact all Methodist groups and compile figures of actual members and also the highest claim as to the total Methodist community." The following statistics are the result. They must be regarded as approximate only.

The membership statistics have been taken from the latest reports and in nearly every case are official. The community figures have been derived from (1) the government census when such was available, (2) the World Christian Handbook, 1952, (3) reports of missionary boards or societies, (4) reports received direct from representatives of the churches, and (5) World Methodist Council estimates.

Considerable diversity exists even in reporting actual members. The British policy is conservative and tends to confine membership within rather strict limits. In the United States the policy is more liberal and the figures include many persons who were formerly classed as "inactive members." However, all are actual members who voluntarily joined the church after reaching "years of accountability" and remain on the church rolls.

The number of those who are otherwise affiliated, or who call themselves Methodists and receive from Methodism all the religious nurture they ever receive, is everywhere much larger than the

membership. This community can only be estimated unless it is revealed in a census, as is the case in Australia, Jamaica, and other
places. In some mission fields, like the Congo, great care is exercised
in admitting members; a large part of an entire tribe may be under
the care of and related to the church while very few are baptized
and communicant members. The community figures include both the
members and the best possible estimate of the number otherwise related to the Methodist churches.

Europe
British Isles

	Membership	Community
Methodist Church in		
Great Britain	783,000	2,500,000
Methodist Church in Ireland	49,000	75,000
Wesleyan Reform Union	6,300	20,000
Independent Methodist		
Churches	9,500	23,000

Continental Europe

Austria	2,000	3,000
Belgium	1,500	2,400
Bulgaria	2,400	5,000
(no recent figures available)		
Czechoslovakia	3,000	4,000
Denmark	3,500	100,000*
Finland	3,000	
France	1,700	2,000
Germany	65,000	105,000
Hungary	1,500	2,500
Italy	4,300	8,000
Norway	9,000	
Poland	12,000	25,000

Portugal	600	1,400
Spain	600	1,000
Sweden	12,000	
Switzerland	15,000	20,000
Yugoslavia	2,000	2,800
	986,900	2,900,100

* Includes Scandinavia and Baltic States

North America

United States of America

	Membership	Community
The Methodist Church	10,409,000	22,500,000
(full members 9,223,000; preparatory members 1,186,000)		
Apostolic Methodist Church	100	200
Congregational Methodist Church	12,000	20,000
Congregational Methodist Church of U.S.A., Inc.	6,500	10,000
Evangelical Methodist Church	5,000	7,000
Free Methodist Church	56,500	139,000
Holiness Methodist Church	700	1,500
New Congregational Methodist Church	1,500	2,500
Primitive Methodist Church	29,000	1,000
Reformed Methodist Church	500	1,000
Reformed New Congregational Methodist Church	500	1,000
Wesleyan Methodist Church of America	36,000	112,500
Southern Methodist Church	6,500	10,000
African Methodist Episcopal Church	1,170,000	2,000,000

African Methodist Episcopal Zion Church	750,000	1,500,000
African Union First Colored Methodist Protestant Church	5,000	7,500
Christian Methodist Church	394,000	500,000
Colored Methodist Protestant Church	200	300
Independent African Methodist Episcopal Church	1,000	1,500
Reformed Zion Union Apostolic Church	13,500	20,000
Reformed Methodist Union Episcopal Church	16,000	25,000
Union American Methodist Episcopal Church	9,400	12,000
Cumberland Methodist Church	60	150
Independent Fundamentalist Methodist University	480	1,000
	12,922,940	26,873,150

Canada

	Membership	Community
United Church of Canada	870,000	1,911,000

(Two-thirds of those entering union in 1925 were Methodists. The community figure is from the Government census.)

Mexico

	Membership	Community
Methodist Church of Mexico	19,000	37,000
Free Methodist Church	950	2,500
Wesleyan Methodist Church, U.S.A.	25	60

Central and South America

	Membership	*Community*
Guatemala		
Primitive Methodist Church	950	2,500
Honduras		
Methodist Church in U.K.	2,500	22,000
Independent Methodist Spanish Honduras	300	3,000
Costa Rica		
Methodist Church in U.K.	400	700
Methodist Church in U.S.A.	650	1,500
Panama Republic and Canal Zone		
Methodist Church in U.K.	1,900	3,500
Methodist Church in U.S.A...........	250	900
Free Methodist Church	100	250
Colombia		
Wesleyan Methodist Church of U.S.A.	150	350
British and Dutch Guiana		
Methodist Church in U.K.	5,500	19,000
African Methodist Episcopal Church	400	700
African Methodist Episcopal Zion Church	600	900
Peru		
Methodist Church in U.S.A...........	1,200	3,000
Bolivia		
Methodist Church in U.S.A.	900	2,700

Brazil

Methodist Church of Brazil	40,000	80,000
Free Methodist Church	350	1,400

Chile

Methodist Church in U.S.A............	7,000	16,000
Methodist Pentecostal and Evangelical Pentecostal, offshoots from Methodism with a Methodist background.....	130,000	250,000

Argentina

Methodist Church in U.S.A............	7,000	11,000

Paraguay

Free Methodist Church	40	380

Uruguay

Methodist Church in U.S.A............	1,900	9,400
	202,090	429,180

West Indies

Bahamas

	Membership	Community
Methodist Church in U.K.	2,800	4,000
African Methodist Episcopal Church	135	250

Cuba

Methodist Church in U.S.A............	8,000	35,000

Jamaica

Methodist Church in U.K............	17,000	100,000 (census)
African Methodist Episcopal Church....	550	1,000

141

Haiti

Methodist Church in U.K.	2,700	8,000
African Methodist Episcopal Church	100	250
Wesleyan Methodist Church, U.S.A.	800	2,000

Dominican Republic

African Methodist Episcopal Church	500	1,800
Free Methodist Church	1,450	5,800
Methodist Church (Union)	1,500	5,000

Puerto Rico

Methodist Church in U.S.A.	12,200	37,000
Wesleyan Meth. Church, U.S.A.	20	50

Lesser Antilles

(British, including Barbados)

Methodist Church in U.K.	20,200	
African Methodist Episcopal Church	300	500
United Church of Canada (two-thirds)	1,750	13,000

Trinidad and Tobago

Methodist Church in U.K.	5,000	
African M.E. Church	400	600
United Church of Canada	20,000	50,000

Leeward Island

(including Antigua, Virgin Is., Curacao, etc.)	15,000	90,000*
African M.E. Church	900	1,200
African M.E.Z. Church	400	600
	111,705	356,050

* Includes British work in Lesser Antilles, Trinidad and Tobago

Asia

Japan

	Membership	Community
Church of Christ in Japan.............	130,000	250,000
(A united church of 133,000 members; the last figures of the Japan Methodist Church are given.)		
Free Methodist Church	3,300	7,900
Wesleyan Methodist Church of U.S.A. ...	100	250

Okinawa

Methodist Church (Union)	3,500	5,000

Korea

Korean Methodist Church	62,000	120,000

Manchuria

Korean Methodist Church	1,500	2,000

China

Methodist Church in U.K.............	45,000	60,000
Methodist Church in U.S.A............	119,000	200,000
Free Methodist Church	3,100	4,200
Wesleyan Methodist Church of U.S.A...	100	250
United Church of Canada	15,000	20,000
(two-thirds including Hong Kong)		

Malaya

Methodist Church in U.S.A............	33,000	75,000

British Borneo (Sarawak)

Methodist Church in U.S.A............	4,000	7,500

Philippine Islands

Methodist Church in U.S.A............	130,000	175,000
Evangelical Methodist Church of Philippines	25,000	70,000
Free Methodist Church	60	570

Sumatra

Methodist Church in U.S.A..........	5,500	12,500

India and Pakistan

Church of South India	171,000	250,000
(Into this church of 244,600 members went from the Methodist Church in U.K.)		
Methodist Church in U.S.A............	800,000	1,500,000
(Full members, 120,000; preparatory members, 260,000; baptized children, 420,000.)		
Methodist Church in North India	3,500	9,000
(Australasian)		
Methodist Church in U.K. (North India)	3,500	8,300
Free Methodist Church	1,000	1,800
Wesleyan Methodist Church of U.S.A...	300	750
United Church of Canada............	20,000	40,000

Burma

Methodist Church in U.K.	3,200	5,300
Methodist Church in U.S.A.	1,500	3,500

Ceylon

Methodist Church in U.K.............	12,000	23,000
	1,596,160	2,851,820

Africa

Algeria and Tunisia

	Membership	Community
Methodist Church in U.S.A.	370	1,000

Ivory Coast

	Membership	Community
Methodist Church in U.K.	25,500	52,500

Dahomey and French Togoland

	Membership	Community
Methodist Church in U.K.	9,500	22,500

Fernando Po

	Membership	Community
Methodist Church in U.K.	700	1,500

Madeira Islands

	Membership	Community
Methodist Church in U.S.A.	5,000	10,000

Gambia

	Membership	Community
Methodist Church in U.K.	1,200	1,800

Sierra Leone

	Membership	Community
Methodist Church in U.K.	9,500	15,000
West African Methodist Church	2,000	2,000
African Methodist Episcopal Church ...	300	500
Wesleyan Methodist Church of U.S.....	500	2,500

Liberia

	Membership	Community
Methodist Church in U.S.A.	22,500	60,000
African Methodist Episcopal Church	1,200	1,500
African Methodist Episcopal Zion Church	2,300	2,500

Gold Coast

	Membership	Community
Methodist Church in U.K.	86,000	151,000
African Methodist Episcopal Church	800	1,000

145

African Methodist Episcopal Zion
Church 4,500 10,000

Nigeria

Methodist Church in U.K. 62,000 114,000
African Methodist Episcopal Church 30,000 30,000
African Methodist Episcopal Zion Church 2,500 10,000

Belgian Congo

Methodist Church in U.S.A. 35,000 100,000
Free Methodist Church 4,800 25,500

Angola

Methodist Church in U.S.A. 19,000 30,000
United Church of Canada 22,000 70,000
   (Angola African Church)
Wesleyan Reform Union 100 100

South Africa

Methodist Church of South Africa...... 545,000 1,025,000*
Methodist Church in U.S.A. 1,000
African Methodist Episcopal Church 35,000
Free Methodist Church 1,200
* Census figures covering all Methodist bodies

Southern Rhodesia

Methodist Church in U.K. 25,000 50,000
Methodist Church in U.S.A. 25,000 75,000
Free Methodist Church 820 2,250

Northern Rhodesia

Methodist Church in U.K. 2,000 3,000
Church of Central Africa 10,000 30,000
   (United Church of Canada)

Mozambique (Portuguese East Africa)

Methodist Church in U.S.A.	9,250	25,000
Free Methodist Church	3,500	11,200
Methodist Church of South Africa	2,700	5,000

Kenya

Methodist Church in U.K.	3,200	7,500
	1,000,740	1,948,850

Australasia

Australia

	Membership	*Community*
Methodist Church of Australasia	350,000	1,000,000
(census, including Fiji Island and Samoa)		

New Zealand

Methodist Church of New Zealand......	37,600	156,000

Indonesia

Methodist Church in U.S.A...........	3,500	10,500

Melanesia (New Guinea, Papua)

Methodist Churches of Australia and N.Z.	10,500	80,000

Solomon Islands

Methodist Church of N.Z............	10,000	17,000

Tonga

Methodist Church of Australia	12,000	25,000

Hawaiian Islands

Methodist Church in U.S.A............	4,000	12,000
	425,000	1,274,500

Totals

Europe

	Membership	Community
British Isles	847,800	2,618,000
Continental Europe	139,100	282,100

Americas

United States of America	12,922,940	26,873,150
Canada	870,000	2,867,000
Mexico	19,975	39,560
Central and South America	202,090	429,180
West Indies	111,705	356,050
Africa	1,000,740	1,948,850
Asia	1,596,160	2,851,820
Australasia	425,000	1,274,500
Grand Total	18,135,510	39,540,210

NOTE: If the formula for estimating adherents used at the Ecumenical Methodist Council at Toronto in 1911 is applied to the above statistics, the results would show 2,480,000 in the former Eastern Section (including Africa and the West Indies), and 49,000,000 in the former Western Section, a total constituency of more than 51,000,000 souls in World Methodism.